You're Invited Back

A Second Helping of
Raleigh's Favorite Recipes

All photography www.tammywingo.com

You're Invited Back

A Second Helping of Raleigh's Favorite Recipes

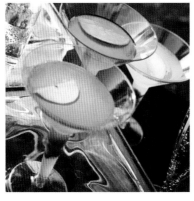

The Junior League of Raleigh

You're Invited Back
A Second Helping of Raleigh's Favorite Recipes

Published by the Junior League of Raleigh, Inc.

Copyright © 2010 by
The Junior League of Raleigh, Inc.
711 Hillsborough Street
Raleigh, North Carolina 27603
919-787-7480

Photography © by Tammy Wingo Photography

This cookbook is a collection of our favorite recipes,
which are not necessarily original recipes.

Library of Congress Control Number: 2009935636
ISBN: 978-0-9631710-6-1

Edited, Designed, and Produced by

Favorite Recipes® Press
an imprint of

FRP.INC

a wholly owned subsidiary of Southwestern/Great American, Inc.
P.O. Box 305142
Nashville, Tennessee 37230
800-358-0560

Art Director and Book Design: Steve Newman
Project Editor: Tanis Westbrook

Manufactured in the United States of America
First Printing: 2010
12,500 copies

Our Mission

The Junior League of Raleigh is an organization of women
committed to promoting voluntarism, developing the potential of women
and improving communities through the effective action and leadership
of trained volunteers.

Our History

Since 1930 the Junior League of Raleigh (JLR) has contributed more than
one million volunteer hours and in excess of $4.8 million to community projects
and programs focusing on education, health needs and children's services.
Our current focus, Promising Youth, places volunteers in strategic
community partnerships across the community.

In 2010 the League opened a new Center for Community Leadership.
The Center for Community Leadership (CCL) serves as a crossroads where
community members and leaders come together to problem solve and spark change.
The CCL is the League's gift to the community, providing much-needed space
and training programs to the many organizations that, like the JLR,
are making a difference in the community.

JUNIOR LEAGUE
OF RALEIGH

Cookbook Development Committee

Co-chairs

Meg Tate Ergenzinger
Sara S. Van Asch

Assistant Co-chairs

Cindy Sparrow Collett
Betsy B. Pittman

Marketing Coordinator

Katie Hammer Johnson

Recipe Coordinators

Chris Trotter Bason
Ellen Greer Buffaloe
Kimberly W. Durland

Tiffany B. Penley
Lisa Venner Price
Jennifer Galioto Strickland

Testing Coordinators

Ann H. Mailly
Leigh Arnemann Peplinski

Committee Members

Tricia Ann Allen
Lauren H. Bell
Sheba Lowe Beverly
Emily J. Brinker
Sarah Anne Calhoun
Tonya Kelsey Chapman
Christy V. Council
Brigid C. Davidson
Ashlegh E. Edwards
Kristen W. Fitzgerald

Susan T. Fountain
Jennifer A. Gwazdauskas
Hunter P. Lemansky
Andrea V. Mace
Melissa Ann McCaskill
Frances S. McClintock
Elisabeth Nixon
Keeley A. Pollard
Sara Allison Reason

Gina Rose Sarant
Samantha C. Saxenmeyer
Danielle R. Slavin
Lauren Davis Tally
Kristen B. Walker
Caroline Coln Wall
Alison Perkins West
Jennifer L. Westcott
Elizabeth Ann Wicker
Katherine Allen Youngblood

Special Thanks

We would like to thank the following people for contributing their
time and expertise during the creation of this book.

Tammy Wingo
Jason Smith
Jeremy Sabo
Rob Bland
Andrew Schaumann
Ian Sullivan

A special thank-you to the staff at Junior League of Raleigh Headquarters,
who assisted with this book more than they may realize.

Tania McLeod, Administrative Director
Melanie Rankin, Development Director
Lori Woods, Administrative Assistant
Joe Wallach, Staff Accountant
Terri Ferraro, Membership Records

Contents

Denotes Junior League of Raleigh favorites

All photography www.tammywingo.com

Menus

You're invited to

You're invited to

A Holiday Brunch

*I*t's the time of year to spend with family and friends,
sharing the holiday spirit with each other.
Prepare this brunch for your guests, and enjoy the warmth of the season.

Old-Fashioned Stollen
page 61

Pecan Praline Bacon
page 64

Sausage Breakfast Casserole with Mushroom Sauce
page 63

Cranberry Apple Bake
page 64

Overnight Bloody Marys
page 44

Citrus Amaretto Coolers
page 43

Orange Coconut Balls
page 176

Coffee and Assorted Juices

All photography www.tammywingo.com

All photography www.tammywingo.com

You're invited to

A Bridesmaids' Luncheon

A bridesmaids' luncheon gathers together some of the most important people in the bride's life right before her wedding day. This menu will satisfy everyone as you celebrate and honor the bride and her family and friends.

Sweet Potato Cups
page 30

City of Oaks Salad with Cranberries and Nuts
page 76

Salmon with Garlic Parmesan Grits
page 115

Raspberry Champagne Punch
page 47

Strawberry Cake with Buttercream Frosting
page 170

You're invited to

A Picnic

The sun is out, the weather is warm and it's the perfect day for a picnic. So pack up a blanket, a good book and some toys for the kids and head out to the park. This menu will help complete the perfect spring day.

Mini Roast Beef Party Sandwiches
page 82

Wild Rice Salad
page 79

Chilled Peach Soup with Amaretto
page 72

Classic Southern Cheese Straws
page 33

White Chocolate Key Lime Cookies
page 173

Pineapple Iced Tea
page 49

Assorted Fruit

All photography www.tammywingo.com

All photography www.tammywingo.co

A Girls' Night Cocktail Party

When was the last time you had a chance to catch up with your girlfriends? Well, tonight is the night! With these great cocktails and plenty of light snacks, prepare to enjoy a great time with friends.

You're invited to
A Fiesta

*Y*ou don't have to wait for Cinco de Mayo for an excuse for a fun Mexican-themed get-together. Invite your friends over for drinks and dinner with this menu that is more than just chips and salsa!

All photography www.tammywingo.com

All photography www.tammywingo.com

You're invited to

Dine al Fresco

Take advantage of the great North Carolina weather by dining outdoors!
This menu will help you move beyond burgers for a party
that is delicious, casual and fun.

BLT Bites
page 32

Bourbon Street Pork Tenderloin
page 94

Marinated Grilled Vegetables
page 149

Fresh Fruit with Honey Mint Sauce
page 80

Parmesan Sesame Bread
page 53

Banana Pudding
page 158

Special Southern Sweet Tea
page 47

You're invited to

An Elegant Dinner Party

*I*t's a chance to spend time with friends and celebrate the special occasions in life.
This dinner menu will create the perfect scene for a wonderful evening as
you and your guests share stories, memories and good cheer.

Mushroom and Goat Cheese Crostini
page 29

Spinach Pistou-Stuffed Beef Tenderloin
page 86

Prosciutto-Wrapped Asparagus
page 32

Carolina Crab Bisque
page 70

Yeast Rolls
page 54

Chocolate Chess Pie with Raspberry Coulis
page 160

Your Favorite Wine

All photography www.tammywingo.com

Appetizers & Beverages

This chapter graciously sponsored by

St. Timothy's School (JK–8th Grade)

Mini Beef Wellingtons

1 sheet frozen puff pastry, thawed
1/3 cup boursin cheese
8 ounces beef tenderloin, trimmed
  and cut into 1/2-inch cubes

Salt and pepper to taste
1 egg, beaten

Preheat the oven to 400 degrees. Roll the puff pastry into a 7 1/2×15-inch rectangle about 1/8 inch thick on lightly floured baking parchment or waxed paper. Cut the pastry into 1 1/2-inch squares. Spoon a scant 1/4 teaspoon of the cheese into the center of each pastry square.

Sprinkle the beef with salt and pepper and place one cube in the center of each square. Fold the pastry to enclose the filling completely, tucking in the edges. Arrange seam side down on a large baking sheet lined with baking parchment.

Brush the pastries with the egg. Bake for 10 to 12 minutes or until puffed and golden brown. Cool slightly on the baking sheet. Remove to a serving platter and serve immediately.

Note: You can freeze the prepared pastries for up to 1 week before baking.

Makes about 48

Photograph for this recipe appears on page 26.

Sausage Cheese Cups

1 pound sausage
1 cup ranch salad dressing
1 (4-ounce) can chopped black olives
1 1/2 cups (6 ounces) shredded
  Monterey Jack cheese

1 1/2 cups (6 ounces) shredded
  Cheddar cheese
1 package won ton wrappers
Sweet chili sauce for dipping

Preheat the oven to 350 degrees. Brown the sausage in a skillet, stirring until crumbly; drain. Combine with the salad dressing, olives, Monterey Jack cheese and Cheddar cheese in a bowl; mix well.

Press the won ton wrappers into greased miniature muffin cups to form cups. Bake for 7 to 8 minutes. Spoon 2 teaspoons of the sausage mixture into each cup. Bake for 10 minutes longer. Serve with sweet chili sauce for dipping.

Makes 48

Brie Quesadillas

1 Vidalia onion, sliced
1 tablespoon extra-virgin olive oil
8 (8-inch) tortillas
4 ounces cream cheese, softened
1/4 wheel Brie cheese, thinly sliced

1 Granny Smith apple, thinly sliced
1 small jar strawberry preserves
3 tablespoons applesauce
Cinnamon to taste

Cook the onion in the olive oil in a sauté pan over low heat until caramelized. Spread the tortillas with a thin layer of the cream cheese. Layer the Brie cheese, apple and caramelized onions on four of the tortillas. Top with the remaining tortillas, placing the cream cheese sides down. Cook on both sides in a skillet sprayed with nonstick cooking spray until the Brie cheese melts.

Mix the strawberry preserves, applesauce and cinnamon in a bowl. Serve with the quesadillas.

Note: You can easily cut the sauce recipe in half as it makes a lot.

Serves 4

Mushroom and Goat Cheese Crostini

1 small baguette
Extra-virgin olive oil for brushing
Salt and pepper to taste
2 tablespoons extra-virgin
    olive oil
1 shallot, thinly sliced into rings

8 ounces wild mushrooms such as
    oyster, portobello, shiitake or
    chanterelle, trimmed and coarsely
    chopped
6 ounces goat cheese, cut into 1/4-inch
    slices and at room temperature
1/4 cup chopped chives

Preheat the oven to 375 degrees. Cut the baguette into 1/4-inch slices and arrange the slices on a baking sheet. Brush with olive oil and season with salt and pepper. Toast for 8 to 10 minutes or until golden brown. Cool to room temperature.

Heat 2 tablespoons olive oil in a skillet over medium heat. Add the shallot and sauté for 3 minutes or until tender. Add the mushrooms. Sauté for 7 to 10 minutes or until very tender and the juices have evaporated. Season with salt and pepper.

Place a slice of goat cheese on each toasted crostini. Top with 1 tablespoon of the mushroom mixture and sprinkle with the chives. Arrange on a serving platter and serve warm.

Serves 4

Sweet Potato Cups

Bacon Vinaigrette
4 slices bacon
1/4 cup minced shallots
2 tablespoons minced garlic
3 tablespoons brown sugar
1/3 cup olive oil
6 tablespoons orange juice
5 tablespoons balsamic vinegar
3 tablespoons Dijon mustard
1/2 teaspoon salt
1/4 teaspoon pepper

Sweet Potato Cups
3 packages miniature frozen phyllo
    shells, thawed
1 1/2 cups (6 ounces) grated
    Parmesan cheese
4 sweet potatoes, peeled and
    finely chopped
2 tablespoons olive oil
1/2 teaspoon salt
1/2 teaspoon pepper
1 package fresh spinach, finely
    chopped
1/2 cup walnuts, coarsely chopped

Vinaigrette

Cook the bacon in a large skillet over medium heat until crisp. Drain the bacon on paper towels and reserve for another use. Reserve two tablespoons of the drippings in the skillet. Add the shallots and garlic to the skillet and sauté for 3 minutes or until tender. Stir in the brown sugar and cook for 1 minute or until the brown sugar dissolves, stirring constantly.

Combine the brown sugar mixture, olive oil, orange juice, vinegar, Dijon mustard, salt and pepper in a food processor or blender; process until smooth. Store in the refrigerator.

Sweet Potato Cups

Preheat the oven to 350 degrees. Arrange the tart shells on a baking sheet sprayed with nonstick cooking spray. Sprinkle about 1 teaspoon of the cheese into each shell. Bake for 10 to 12 minutes or until light brown. Cool to room temperature.

Increase the oven temperature to 400 degrees. Combine the sweet potatoes, olive oil, salt and pepper in a large bowl and toss to coat evenly. Spread in a single layer on a large baking sheet. Roast for 20 to 25 minutes or just until the sweet potatoes are fork-tender. Cool in the pan for 10 to 15 minutes. Remove to a bowl and cool to room temperature.

Place the desired amount of vinaigrette in a microwave-safe bowl. Microwave on High for 10 to 20 seconds or until heated through. Combine with the spinach and mix well. Spoon into the phyllo shells. Top with the sweet potato mixture and sprinkle with the walnuts.

Store any unused vinaigrette in the refrigerator to use as a salad dressing. The phyllo shells and sweet potato mixture can be prepared in advance. Store the shells in an airtight container and the sweet potato mixture in the refrigerator in an airtight container. Bring the sweet potatoes to room temperature before serving.

Makes 45

Shrimp and Grits Tarts

Shrimp Gravy

2 pounds shrimp
Salt to taste
6 tablespoons lemon juice
Pepper to taste
6 slices bacon, finely chopped
1 small onion, finely chopped
2/3 cup finely chopped green or
    red bell pepper
2 garlic cloves, minced
2 1/2 tablespoons all-purpose flour
1 cup chicken stock

Shrimp and Grits Tarts

1 1/4 cups chicken stock
1 cup heavy cream
1/4 cup (1/2 stick) butter
Salt and pepper to taste
2 1/2 cups quick-cooking grits
2 cups (8 ounces) shredded sharp
    Cheddar cheese
Hot sauce to taste

Gravy

Peel and devein the shrimp, reserving the shells. Combine the shells with lightly salted water in a saucepan. Simmer over medium-low heat for 10 to 12 minutes. Strain, discarding the shells. Reserve 1/2 cup of the stock for the gravy and 1 1/4 cups of the stock for the grits; keep warm.

Cut each shrimp into three or four pieces. Sprinkle with the lemon juice, salt and pepper in a bowl. Fry the bacon in a large skillet over medium heat until brown but not crisp. Add the onion, bell pepper and garlic. Sauté for 10 minutes or until the onion is translucent. Sprinkle with the flour and cook for 1 minute, stirring constantly. Stir in the chicken stock and reserved 1/2 cup shrimp stock. Season with salt. Cook for 5 minutes longer, stirring frequently.

Tarts

Combine 1 1/4 cups reserved shrimp stock, the chicken stock, cream, butter, salt and pepper in a large saucepan. Bring to a gentle boil over medium-high heat. Add the grits gradually, stirring constantly. Reduce the heat to medium-low and cook for 5 minutes or until the liquid is absorbed and the grits are tender and have the consistency of thick oatmeal.

Stir in the cheese, hot sauce and shrimp gravy. Spoon immediately into greased miniature muffin cups. Chill, covered, until firm.

Preheat the oven to 375 degrees. Remove the chilled tarts from the muffin cups and place on a baking sheet. Bake until heated through. Sprinkle with additional cheese, if desired.

You can also pour the grits 3/4 inch thick in a shallow dish and chill. Cut into the desired shapes and heat to serve.

Makes about 125

Prosciutto-Wrapped Asparagus

40 spears fresh asparagus, about 1¹/₂ pounds
40 thin slices prosciutto, about 8 ounces
2 tablespoons extra-virgin olive oil
2 tablespoons fresh lemon juice

Preheat the oven to 450 degrees. Wrap each asparagus spear with one slice of prosciutto. Arrange on a foil-lined baking sheet. Brush with the olive oil and drizzle with the lemon juice. Roast for 8 to 10 minutes or until the prosciutto is crisp. Serve immediately.

Makes 40

Photograph for this recipe appears on page 26.

BLT Bites

20 cherry tomatoes
1 pound bacon, crisp-cooked
   and crumbled
¹/₃ cup chopped green onions
¹/₂ cup mayonnaise or mayonnaise-
   type salad dressing

3 tablespoons grated Parmesan cheese
   or crumbled blue cheese
2 tablespoons finely chopped
   fresh parsley

Cut a thin slice from the top of each tomato; scoop out and discard the center. Cut a thin slice from the bottom to help them sit up straight. Invert the tomatoes on a paper towel to drain.

Combine the bacon, green onions, mayonnaise, cheese and parsley in a small bowl and mix well. Spoon into the tomatoes and arrange on a serving plate. Chill for several hours before serving.

Serves 10

Photograph for this recipe appears on page 139.

Blue Cheese Chips

4 ounces blue cheese, crumbled
3 tablespoons tub-style cream
   cheese, softened
1/3 cup whipping cream
1 (5-ounce) package crinkle-cut
   potato chips (tested with
   kettle-cooked)

1 cup chopped walnuts, toasted
2 teaspoons chopped fresh thyme
2 teaspoons chopped fresh rosemary
3 tablespoons bottled
   balsamic glaze

Preheat the oven to 400 degrees. Combine the blue cheese, cream cheese and cream in a bowl and mix until smooth. Spread the potato chips on a baking parchment-lined baking sheet, making two layers if necessary. Dollop the cheese mixture over the chips and sprinkle with the walnuts. Bake for 5 minutes. Slide the chips onto a serving platter. Sprinkle with the thyme and rosemary and drizzle with the balsamic glaze. Serve immediately.

   Note: Do not substitute balsamic vinegar for the balsamic glaze. You can make your own glaze by mixing 3 tablespoons sugar with 1/2 cup balsamic vinegar in a saucepan or microwave-safe bowl. Cook on the stovetop or in the microwave until reduced enough to coat the back of a spoon.

Serves 8 to 10

Classic Southern Cheese Straws

3 cups all-purpose flour
1/2 teaspoon baking powder
1/2 teaspoon salt
1/2 teaspoon cayenne pepper, or
   to taste

1 1/2 pounds Cheddar cheese,
   finely shredded and
   at room temperature
1 cup (2 sticks) butter, softened

Preheat the oven to 325 degrees. Mix the flour, baking powder, salt and cayenne pepper together. Combine the cheese and butter in a mixing bowl and beat until smooth. Add the flour mixture gradually, beating until well mixed after each addition. Spoon into a cookie press fitted with a small star tip.

   Press the cheese mixture into long strips on a greased baking sheet. Bake for 13 minutes or until light golden brown; do not overbake. Cut into the desired lengths while hot. Remove to wire racks to cool. Store in an airtight container.

   Do not substitute margarine for the butter in this recipe.

Makes 12 dozen

Black Mussel Ceviche

Onion Salsa
2 red onions, minced

2 garlic cloves, minced

4 or 5 mild banana peppers or mild
  Hungarian peppers, minced

1/2 bunch cilantro, minced

Juice of 5 lemons

Splash of olive oil

1/4 to 1/2 teaspoon Peruvian yellow
  hot pepper paste (optional)

Black Mussel Ceviche
1 (2- to 3-pound) bag
  black mussels

1 lemon

1/2 bunch cilantro

Salt to taste

Lettuce leaves

1 jar chopped pimentos, drained

Salsa

Combine the onions, garlic, banana peppers, cilantro, lemon juice, olive oil and hot pepper paste in a bowl and mix well. Chill, covered, in the refrigerator.

Ceviche

Immerse the mussels in cold water and scrub well, changing the water as needed. Remove the beard on the sides of the mussels using a knife and scissors. Fill a large saucepan with water. Squeeze the juice of the lemon into the saucepan and add the lemon. Add two sprigs of the cilantro and season with salt. Bring to a boil and add the mussels. Cook until the mussels begin to open. Cook for 2 minutes longer and then drain onto a platter, discarding any shells that do not open. Cool to room temperature.

Open the shells carefully with a paring knife. Remove the mussels from the shells. Separate the halves of the mussel shells, reserving half of each shell. Cut out and discard the small piece of mussel that is attached to each reserved shell. Arrange the reserved shells on a plate lined with lettuce. Place one mussel in each shell and top with the onion salsa. Chill, covered, in the refrigerator for 3 hours.

Top each mussel with one piece of pimento and one cilantro leaf. Garnish the center of the plate with the remaining cilantro bunch. Let stand at room temperature for 15 to 20 minutes before serving.

Note: You can also mix the mussels with the onion salsa in a bowl and chill for 3 hours. Spoon into the reserved mussel shells and garnish as above. Peruvian yellow hot pepper paste is also known as aji and can be found in Latin markets.

Serves 4

Rosemary Roasted Cashews

1¹/2 pounds roasted unsalted cashews
3 tablespoons minced fresh
   rosemary leaves
2 tablespoons butter, melted

1 tablespoon dark brown sugar
¹/2 teaspoon ground coriander
2 teaspoons kosher salt
¹/2 teaspoon red pepper

Preheat the oven to 375 degrees. Spread the cashews on a baking sheet. Roast for 10 minutes. Combine the rosemary with the butter, brown sugar, coriander, salt and red pepper in a large bowl. Add the cashews and toss to coat well. Serve warm.

Makes 3 cups

Photograph for this recipe appears on page 26.

Almond Bacon Cheese

8 ounces Cheddar cheese, shredded
8 ounces white Cheddar cheese,
   shredded
1 cup chopped green onions with tops

1 pound bacon, crisp-cooked
   and crumbled
1 cup toasted slivered almonds
1 cup (or less) mayonnaise

Combine the Cheddar cheese, white Cheddar cheese, green onions, bacon and almonds in a bowl. Add the mayonnaise gradually, mixing until the desired consistency is reached. Chill for 2 hours or longer before serving with crackers or on baked potatoes or hamburgers. Add additional mayonnaise at serving time if needed.

Serves 24

Hostess: host·ess n. A woman who receives or entertains guests in a social or official capacity.

Black Bean Hummus

1 (15-ounce) can black beans, drained
   and rinsed
1/2 cup cilantro
1 teaspoon minced garlic
Juice of 1 lime
1/2 teaspoon hot pepper sauce

1/2 teaspoon ground cumin
1/2 teaspoon crushed red pepper
1/4 teaspoon cayenne pepper
1/4 cup olive oil
Salt and black pepper to taste

Combine the beans, cilantro, garlic, lime juice, hot sauce, cumin, red pepper and cayenne pepper in a food processor. Add the olive oil gradually, processing constantly until smooth and creamy. Season with salt and black pepper. Serve with pita chips.

Serves 4 to 6

Cranberry Pepper Jelly Cheese Ball

3 ounces hot red pepper jelly
8 ounces whole cranberry sauce
24 ounces cream cheese, softened
1/2 cup chopped pecans

1/2 tablespoon dried dill weed
2 cups chopped pecans
1 tablespoon dried dill weed

Melt the jelly in a small saucepan. Combine with the cranberry sauce, cream cheese, 1/2 cup pecans and 1/2 tablespoon dill weed in a mixing bowl; mix well. Line a bowl with plastic wrap and spoon the cream cheese mixture into the bowl. Round off the top of the cream cheese mixture and cover with the plastic wrap. Chill in the refrigerator.

Combine 2 cups pecans and 1 tablespoon dill weed on waxed paper. Remove the cheese ball from the bowl with the plastic wrap. Remove the plastic wrap and roll the cheese ball in the pecan mixture. Place on a serving plate and serve with crackers.

Serves 24

Roquefort and Avocado Spread

1 cup crumbled Roquefort cheese
1/2 cup sour cream
2 avocados, mashed
2 tablespoons finely sliced scallions

1/2 cup bottled sliced jalapeño chiles
1/4 teaspoon paprika
Blue corn chips

Combine the cheese and sour cream in a bowl and mix well. Add the avocados, scallions and jalapeño chiles; mix well. Spoon into the center of a serving dish and sprinkle with the paprika. Serve with blue corn chips.

Serves 4 to 6

Slightly Spicy Pimento Cheese

1 (16-ounce) block sharp
   Cheddar cheese
1 (16-ounce) block Pepper
   Jack cheese

1 onion
1 (4-ounce) jar chopped
   pimentos, drained
Mayonnaise (optional)

Place a hand grater in a medium or large bowl and grate the Cheddar cheese and Pepper Jack cheese into the bowl. Grate the onion into the bowl using the smallest openings on the grater. Add the pimentos and mix well; the mixture will be loose. Add mayonnaise only if necessary to bind the mixture. Serve with vegetables or crackers as a dip or spread or use as a spread for sandwiches.

Serves 12 to 16

Baked Blue Cheese Artichoke Dip

1 (14-ounce) can artichoke
    hearts, drained
8 ounces cream cheese, softened
1 cup crumbled blue cheese

$1/2$ cup (2 ounces) shredded
    Parmesan cheese
1 cup mayonnaise
$1/2$ cup sliced green onions

Preheat the oven to 350 degrees. Combine the artichoke hearts, cream cheese, blue cheese, Parmesan cheese, mayonnaise and green onions in a food processor. Process until mixed but not completely smooth. Spoon into a 9-inch pie plate. Bake for 20 to 25 minutes or until light brown. Let stand for 5 to 10 minutes before serving. Serve with crackers.

Serves 16

Caliente Corn Dip

2 tablespoons butter
$1/4$ cup chopped onion
2 tablespoons chopped jalapeño chiles
$1^1/2$ tablespoons minced garlic
3 cups fresh, canned or frozen white
    corn kernels
1 cup chopped roasted red peppers
4 ounces Cheddar cheese, shredded

4 ounces Monterey Jack cheese,
    shredded
$3/4$ cup light sour cream
$3/4$ cup light mayonnaise
$1/4$ cup finely chopped green
    onion tops
Paprika, seasoned salt and cayenne
    pepper to taste

Melt the butter in a 10-inch sauté pan over medium-high heat. Add the onion and sauté until tender. Add the jalapeño chiles and garlic and sauté for 2 minutes. Stir in the corn and sauté for 6 minutes.

Spoon the corn mixture into a bowl and add the roasted red peppers, Cheddar cheese, Monterey Jack cheese, sour cream, mayonnaise, green onion tops, paprika, seasoned salt and cayenne pepper; mix well.

Preheat the oven to 375 degrees. Spoon the dip into a baking dish. Bake for 20 minutes or until bubbly. Serve with corn chips.

Serves 8

Deacon Dip

2 tablespoons balsamic vinegar
3 tablespoons vegetable oil
Sugar to taste
1 (15-ounce) can black beans,
　　drained and rinsed

1 (15-ounce) can Shoe Peg corn or
　　white corn, drained
1 (10-ounce) can tomatoes with
　　green chiles, partially drained
4 ounces feta cheese, crumbled

Mix the vinegar, oil and a small amount of sugar in a small bowl. Combine the beans, corn, tomatoes with green chiles and cheese in a large bowl; mix well. Add the dressing and toss to coat well. Store in the refrigerator for 8 hours or longer to blend the flavors, stirring occasionally. Bring to room temperature to serve. Serve with tortilla chips.

Serves 16

Rockin' Guacamole

4 avocados
2 Roma tomatoes, chopped
1 small sweet onion, chopped
2 tablespoons lemon juice
1 tablespoon ground cumin
1 teaspoon garlic powder, or
　　to taste

1 teaspoon chili powder
1/4 cup mayonnaise or light
　　mayonnaise
1/2 cup sour cream or light
　　sour cream
3 dashes of Tabasco sauce, or to taste
Salt to taste

Mash the avocados with a potato masher in a large bowl. Add the tomatoes, onion, lemon juice, cumin, garlic powder and chili powder; mix well. Stir in the mayonnaise and sour cream. Season with the Tabasco sauce and salt. Serve immediately or cover with foil and store in the refrigerator until serving time. Serve with chips.

Serves 4 to 6

Harvest Pumpkin Dip

8 ounces reduced-fat cream
   cheese, softened
2 cups confectioners' sugar

1 (15-ounce) can pumpkin pie filling
1 1/2 teaspoons cinnamon
3/4 teaspoon ginger

Combine the cream cheese and confectioners' sugar in a mixing bowl and beat at medium speed until smooth. Add the pie filling, cinnamon and ginger; mix well. Chill, covered, in the refrigerator for 8 hours or longer. Serve with gingersnaps and sliced Granny Smith apples. You can also serve it as a spread for a bagel.

Serves 6 to 8

Baked Spinach Dip

1 onion, chopped
1 garlic clove, minced
Butter for sautéing
1 (15-ounce) can diced
   tomatoes, drained
8 ounces cream cheese, softened
1/2 cup mayonnaise
1/3 cup sour cream
1 (4-ounce) can black olives,
   chopped

1 or 2 tablespoons chopped canned
   jalapeño chiles
1 1/2 cups (6 ounces) shredded
   Mexican cheese
1 (10-ounce) package frozen chopped
   spinach, thawed and well drained
1/2 cup (2 ounces) shredded
   Mexican cheese
1 package 6-inch flour tortillas,
   cut into triangles and warmed

Preheat the oven to 350 degrees. Sauté the onion and garlic in a small amount of butter in a saucepan until tender. Add the tomatoes and cook for 2 minutes longer. Cool to room temperature.

Combine the onion mixture with the cream cheese, mayonnaise and sour cream in a bowl; mix well. Add the olives, jalapeño chiles and 1 1/2 cups cheese; mix well. Stir in the spinach. Spoon the spinach mixture into a baking dish and top with 1/2 cup cheese. Bake for 30 minutes or until bubbly. Serve with the warm tortillas.

Serves 8 to 10

Spinach and Hearts of Palm Dip

22 (6-inch) corn tortillas
Salt to taste
1 (10-ounce) package frozen
    chopped spinach, thawed
    and well drained
1 (14-ounce) can hearts of palm,
    drained and chopped
1 tablespoon minced fresh garlic
$1/2$ cup low-fat or fat-free sour cream

8 ounces low-fat cream
    cheese, softened
1 (6-ounce) container light garlic and
    herb cheese spread, softened
$1^1/4$ cups (5 ounces) shredded
    part-skim mozzarella cheese
$1/2$ cup (2 ounces) grated
    asiago cheese
Grated Parmesan cheese to taste

Preheat the oven to 375 degrees. Cut each tortilla into eight wedges. Arrange the wedges in a single layer on a baking sheet sprayed with nonstick cooking spray. Lightly coat the wedges with olive oil spray and sprinkle with salt. Bake for 15 minutes or until crisp and light brown.

Reduce the oven temperature to 350 degrees. Combine the spinach, hearts of palm, garlic, sour cream, cream cheese, cheese spread, mozzarella cheese and half the asiago cheese in a bowl; mix well.

Spoon the mixture into a baking dish sprayed with nonstick cooking spray. Top with the remaining asiago cheese and Parmesan cheese. Bake for 40 minutes or until bubbly and light brown. Serve warm with the tortilla wedges.

Serves 22

Citrus Amaretto Coolers

1 (12-ounce) can frozen lemonade
    concentrate, thawed
1 (12-ounce) can frozen orange juice
    concentrate, thawed

9 cups water
3 cups amaretto
1 (16-ounce) jar maraschino cherries
Ginger ale (optional)

Combine the lemonade concentrate and orange juice concentrate in a large freezer container and stir to mix well. Add the water, amaretto and undrained cherries. Freeze until slushy. Spoon into individual glasses and add ginger ale. Store in the freezer.

Serves 32

Overnight Bloody Marys

1 (48-ounce) can vegetable
    juice cocktail
1 (48-ounce) can tomato juice
1 cup lemon juice
2 tablespoons Worcestershire sauce

1 teaspoon salt
1/2 teaspoon seasoned salt
3 cups vodka
Celery stalks or shrimp cocktail
    skewers for garnish

Combine the vegetable juice cocktail, tomato juice, lemon juice, Worcestershire sauce, salt and seasoned salt in a large pitcher; mix well. Chill in the refrigerator for 8 hours or longer. Stir in the vodka at serving time. Serve over ice with a celery stalk or shrimp cocktail skewer.

Serves 12

Photograph for this recipe appears on page 26.

Mucho Margaritas

1 (12-ounce) can frozen
    lemonade concentrate
1 (12-ounce) can frozen
    limeade concentrate
1 cup confectioners' sugar

8 cups ice
3 liters ginger ale, chilled
3 cups tequila
3 limes, thinly sliced
Margarita salt

Combine the lemonade concentrate, limeade concentrate and confectioners' sugar in a pitcher. Pour half the juice mixture into a blender and add half the ice or enough to fill the blender. Process until smooth; pour into a large pitcher or tea dispenser. Repeat the process with the remaining juice mixture and ice. Add the ginger ale and tequila and mix well. Top with the lime slices and serve in glasses with rims dipped in margarita salt.

Serves 28

What is there more kindly than the feeling between host and guest? —Aeschylus

Pomegranate Margaritas

1 lime, cut into quarters
Coarse salt
1/2 cup pomegranate juice
1/2 cup tequila

1/2 cup Cointreau
1/4 cup fresh lime juice
1/4 cup confectioners' sugar
6 cups ice

Rub the rims of margarita glasses with the cut lime and dip into coarse salt to coat the rims. Combine the pomegranate juice, tequila, Cointreau, lime juice and confectioners' sugar in a blender. Add the ice and process until smooth. Serve in the prepared glasses.

Serves 4 to 6

Mojo Mojitos

1 lime, cut into quarters
Sugar for coating the rims
Juice and pulp of 10 limes
3/4 cup sugar

25 to 30 fresh mint leaves
1 cup white rum
Club soda, chilled

Rub the rims of cocktail glasses with the cut lime and dip into sugar to coat the rims. Combine the lime juice and pulp with 3/4 cup sugar and the mint leaves in a pitcher. Stir with a wooden spoon or muddler to release the mint oil. Add the rum and desired amount of club soda and ice. Serve in the prepared glasses.

Note: You can prepare the basic mixture in advance and store, covered, in the refrigerator. Add the club soda and ice at serving time or serve over ice in glasses, allowing the guests to add the desired amount of club soda.

Serves 8 to 10

Raleighwood Pink Melon-tini

2 cups watermelon purée
1 cup fresh lemon juice
1 cup vodka

1 cup water
1/2 cup sugar
Mint leaves, for garnish

Combine the watermelon purée, lemon juice, vodka, water and sugar in a pitcher and mix well to dissolve the sugar. Serve over ice in glasses. Garnish with mint leaves.

Serves 6

Pink Pear

1 1/4 cups pink lemonade
1 1/4 cups pear vodka
4 lemon slices, for garnish

Mix the lemonade and vodka in a pitcher. Serve over ice in cocktail glasses. Garnish with lemon slices.

Serves 4

Topsail Spritzer

1 1/2 ounces citron vodka
Seltzer water
Diet lemon-lime soda

Juice of 1 lemon wedge
1 lemon wedge, for garnish

Fill a cocktail glass with ice and add the vodka. Add equal amounts of seltzer water and lemon-lime soda. Add the lemon juice to the drink and mix gently. Garnish with the lemon wedge.

Serves 1

Special Southern Sweet Tea

3/4 cup iced tea
3 tablespoons vodka
2 tablespoons simple syrup
1 or 2 sprigs of fresh mint

Combine the iced tea, vodka, simple syrup and mint in a tall glass and mix gently. Add ice and serve.

Serves 1

Raspberry Champagne Punch

1 liter lemon-lime soda
2 (750-milliliter) bottles Champagne
1 gallon raspberry sherbet
Chambord
Raspberries, for garnish

Combine the lemon-lime soda, Champagne and sherbet in a punch bowl and mix gently. Ladle into Champagne glasses and add a splash of Chambord to each glass. Garnish with raspberries.

Serves 10

Raleigh is the largest city in a metropolitan area known as the Research Triangle.

Fruit Punch

16 cups (4 quarts) cranberry juice
1 (12-ounce) can frozen lemonade
   concentrate, thawed
1 (48-ounce) container orange juice

1 (46-ounce) can pineapple juice
2 liters lemon-lime soda
Orange slices and lemon slices,
   for garnish

Pour half the cranberry juice into a ring mold and freeze until firm. Combine the remaining cranberry juice with the lemonade concentrate, orange juice and pineapple juice in a punch bowl and mix well. Add the lemon-lime soda and frozen cranberry juice mold at serving time. Garnish with orange slices and lemon slices.

Serves 50

Party Punch

2 cups water
2 large packages flavored gelatin
   of choice
3 cups sugar

2 cups cold water
1 (46-ounce) can pineapple juice
1/2 cup lemon juice
2 (2-liter) bottles ginger ale, chilled

Bring 2 cups water to a boil in a large saucepan and add the gelatin and sugar; stir to dissolve the gelatin and sugar completely. Stir in 2 cups cold water, the pineapple juice and lemon juice. Pour into a plastic freezer container and freeze until needed. Let stand at room temperature until slushy. Combine with the ginger ale in a punch bowl and mix gently. Serve in punch cups.

Note: You can freeze a small amount of the punch base in a separate smaller container to add to the punch to keep it chilled as it is served.

Serves 50

Piña Colada Punch

1 (46-ounce) can unsweetened
    pineapple juice, chilled
2 cups piña colada cocktail
    mix, chilled
1 (12-ounce) can frozen orange juice
    concentrate, thawed and chilled

1 liter ginger ale, chilled
1 liter lemon-lime soda, chilled
1 (10-ounce) package frozen
    raspberries in syrup,
    partially thawed

Combine the pineapple juice, cocktail mix, orange juice concentrate, ginger ale and lemon-lime soda in a punch bowl and mix well. Add the raspberries and mix gently. Serve chilled in punch cups.

Serves 24

Fresh-Squeezed Lemonade

1/2 cup water
1 1/2 cups sugar or equivalent amount
    of sugar substitute

5 cups cold water
1 1/2 cups fresh lemon juice
1 tablespoon grated lemon zest

Bring 1/2 cup water to a boil in a small saucepan. Add to the sugar in a pitcher and stir to dissolve the sugar completely. Add 5 cups cold water, the lemon juice and lemon zest and mix well. Chill in the refrigerator. Serve over ice.

Serves 10

Pineapple Iced Tea

16 cups (1 gallon) water
2 1/2 cups sugar
4 family-size tea bags

1 (46-ounce) cans unsweetened
    pineapple juice
1 cup fresh lemon juice

Combine the water and sugar in a large saucepan and bring to a boil, stirring to dissolve the sugar completely. Remove from the heat and add the tea bags; let steep for 10 minutes. Remove the tea bags and let stand for 10 minutes. Stir in the pineapple juice and lemon juice. Serve over ice.

Note: You can purchase a gallon of water for ease of measurement and for a container in which to store the tea.

Serves 10

All photography www.tammywingo.com

Breads & Breakfast

This chapter graciously sponsored by **Belk**

Lemon Rosemary Focaccia with Caramelized Onions

2 tablespoons extra-virgin olive oil
1 large sweet onion, thinly sliced
1 tablespoon water
1/2 teaspoon chopped fresh thyme
Salt to taste
1 pound frozen pizza dough, thawed
Extra-virgin olive oil

1 1/2 teaspoons finely chopped
   fresh rosemary
Coarsely ground pepper to taste
1/2 thin-skinned lemon, very
   thinly sliced
1/2 teaspoon coarse sea salt

Heat 2 tablespoons olive oil in a large skillet. Add the onion, water and thyme; season with salt. Cook over low heat for 1 hour or until the onion is very tender and golden brown, stirring occasionally. Cool to room temperature.

Place a pizza stone on the bottom rack of the oven and preheat the oven to 425 degrees for 30 minutes. Roll or press the pizza dough into an 11-inch circle on a lightly floured surface. Remove to a baking sheet lined with baking parchment and reshape if necessary. Prick all over with a fork.

Brush the dough with olive oil and sprinkle with the rosemary and pepper. Arrange the lemon slices over the dough and brush with olive oil. Top with the caramelized onions. Cover with plastic wrap and let rise for 15 minutes.

Remove the plastic wrap and slide the dough and baking parchment onto the heated pizza stone. Bake for 25 minutes or until puffed and brown. Brush with olive oil and sprinkle evenly with the sea salt. Cut into wedges and serve hot.

Serves 8

RSVP: *The term RSVP comes from the French expression "répondez s'il vous plaît," meaning "please respond." If RSVP is written on an invitation it means the invited guest must tell the host whether or not he or she plans to attend the party. It does not mean to respond only if you're coming, and it does not mean to respond only if you're not coming (the expression "regrets only" is reserved for that instance).*

Parmesan Sesame Bread

1/4 cup (1 ounce) grated
    Parmesan cheese
3 tablespoons sesame seeds
1 teaspoon dried basil

3 tablespoons butter or
    margarine, melted
1 (25-ounce) package frozen
    roll dough

Mix the cheese, sesame seeds and basil together. Spoon one-third of the cheese mixture and 1 tablespoon of the butter into a lightly oiled bundt pan.

Arrange half the rolls in the prepared pan. Sprinkle with half the remaining cheese mixture and drizzle with half the remaining butter. Arrange the remaining rolls in the pan and top with the remaining cheese mixture and butter. Let rise in a warm place for 2 hours.

Preheat the oven to 350 degrees. Bake the bread for 20 minutes. Cover with foil and bake for 10 minutes longer. Invert onto a serving plate and serve warm.

To prepare this in muffin cups, reduce the baking time to 15 to 20 minutes.

Serves 8 to 10

Jack Bread

1 large loaf French bread
3/4 cup (1 1/2 sticks) margarine
1 tablespoon chopped fresh parsley
1 teaspoon dried minced onion flakes

1 teaspoon poppy seeds
1/8 teaspoon pepper
16 ounces Monterey Jack cheese,
    sliced

Preheat the oven to 350 degrees. Slice the French bread, cutting three-fourths of the way through. Combine the margarine, parsley, onion flakes, poppy seeds and pepper in a small saucepan. Heat over low heat until the margarine melts, stirring to mix well. Brush on each slice of the bread with a pastry brush. Place one slice of cheese between each slice of the bread.

Wrap the bread in foil and bake for 15 minutes. Open the foil and bake for 15 minutes longer or until light brown.

Serves 6 to 8

Quick Blue Cheese Rolls

2 (8-count) cans refrigerator
    flaky biscuits

1 cup (2 sticks) butter
4 to 6 ounces blue cheese, crumbled

Preheat the oven to 350 degrees. Separate the biscuits and cut each biscuit into quarters. Place the butter and cheese on a rimmed baking sheet. Bake for 4 to 5 minutes or until melted. Stir to blend well. Add the biscuit pieces and toss to coat evenly. Bake for 8 to 12 minutes or until golden brown. Brush the tops with the butter and cheese mixture remaining on the baking sheet and serve warm.

Makes 32

Yeast Rolls

1 cup shortening
3/4 cup sugar
2 teaspoons salt
1 cup boiling water
2 envelopes dry yeast

1 teaspoon sugar
1 cup warm water
2 eggs, lightly beaten
6 cups all-purpose flour

Combine the shortening, 3/4 cup sugar and the salt in a bowl. Add 1 cup boiling water and stir to melt the shortening and dissolve the sugar. Cool to room temperature.

Sprinkle the yeast and 1 teaspoon sugar over 1 cup warm water in a bowl and let stand for 10 minutes. Add to the shortening mixture. Add the eggs and flour; mix well to form a dough. Let rise, covered, in the refrigerator for 4 hours.

Roll the dough 1/2 inch thick on a lightly floured surface. Cut with a round cutter and arrange in greased round pans, leaving a small space between the rolls. Let rise in a warm place for 30 minutes.

Preheat the oven to 350 degrees. Bake the rolls for 10 to 12 minutes or until golden brown.

Makes 2 dozen

Banana Bread

2 cups all-purpose flour
1 teaspoon baking powder
1 teaspoon baking soda
1 teaspoon salt
1/2 cup (1 stick) butter, softened
1 cup sugar
2 eggs
1 tablespoon banana flavoring

1 tablespoon vanilla extract
2 cups mashed overripe bananas
2 cups (12 ounces) semisweet
    chocolate chips, milk chocolate
    chips and/or butterscotch chips
1 cup pecans, finely chopped
Chocolate chips for topping
    (optional)

Preheat the oven to 350 degrees. Mix the flour, baking powder, baking soda and salt together. Cream the butter and sugar in a mixing bowl until light and fluffy. Beat in the eggs one at a time. Add the flavorings and mix well. Add the dry ingredients and mix well. Beat in the bananas. Stir in 2 cups chocolate chips and half the pecans.

Spoon the batter into a greased and floured 5×9-inch loaf pan. Sprinkle with the remaining pecans and additional chocolate chips. Bake for 50 minutes. Cool in the pan for 5 minutes and remove to a wire rack to cool completely.

Note: You can also use peanut butter chips, swirl chips or white chocolate chips.

Serves 16

Spiced Pumpkin Bread

1 2/3 cups self-rising flour
1 1/2 cups sugar
1 teaspoon baking soda
1/4 teaspoon baking powder
1 teaspoon cinnamon
1 teaspoon ground cloves
1/2 teaspoon nutmeg

3/4 teaspoon salt
2 eggs, beaten
1/2 cup vegetable oil
1/2 cup water
1 (15-ounce) can pumpkin
1/2 cup chopped pecans (optional)

Preheat the oven to 325 degrees. Mix the flour, sugar, baking soda, baking powder, cinnamon, cloves, nutmeg and salt in a mixing bowl. Add the eggs, oil, water and pumpkin; beat until smooth. Stir in the pecans.

Spray two loaf pans or a bundt pan with nonstick cooking spray. Spoon the batter into the pans. Bake for 50 minutes or until a wooden pick inserted into the center comes out clean. Cool in the pans for 5 minutes and remove to a wire rack to cool completely.

Serves 12 to 15

Zesty Corn Bread

1 cup cornmeal
1 teaspoon baking soda
1/2 cup buttermilk
3 eggs
1 (15-ounce) can cream-style corn

2 tablespoons chopped onion
4 to 8 ounces sharp Cheddar cheese,
    shredded
3 hot chiles, chopped

Preheat the oven to 350 degrees. Heat a greased iron skillet until hot. Combine the cornmeal, baking soda, buttermilk, eggs, corn and onion in a bowl and mix well. Pour half the batter into the heated skillet. Sprinkle with the cheese and chiles. Add the remaining batter. Bake for 45 to 50 minutes or until golden brown. Cut into wedges to serve.

Serves 6 to 8

Quick and Incredible Cheese Biscuits

2 cups (8 ounces) shredded sharp
    Cheddar cheese
1 cup (2 sticks) butter, melted

1 cup sour cream
2 cups self-rising flour

Preheat the oven to 350 degrees. Mix the cheese and butter in a bowl; cool for 2 minutes. Add the sour cream and mix well. Stir in the flour. Spoon into greased miniature muffin cups. Bake for 18 to 22 minutes or until golden brown.

Note: You can mix 1/2 teaspoon garlic powder or 1/2 teaspoon cayenne pepper with the flour. Or you can combine the butter and sour cream with a mixture of the flour and 2 teaspoons dried dill seeds; after baking, brush the biscuits with 2 tablespoons melted butter and sprinkle with 1 teaspoon dried dill weed.

Makes 40

Volunteers don't get paid, not because they're worthless, but because they're priceless.   —Sherry Anderson

Peach Muffins with Peach Butter

Peach Butter
1/2 cup (1 stick) unsalted
  butter, softened
1/4 cup peach preserves

Peach Muffins
1 1/2 cups all-purpose flour
1/2 cup sugar
1 1/2 teaspoons baking powder
1/2 teaspoon baking soda
1/2 teaspoon salt

1 cup chopped fresh peaches or
  thawed frozen unsweetened
  peaches
1 tablespoon all-purpose flour
1 cup sour cream
1/4 cup (1/2 stick) butter, melted
1 egg
1/2 teaspoon vanilla extract
1/8 teaspoon almond extract
Sugar for sprinkling

Butter
Combine the butter and preserves in a medium bowl and mix well with a rubber spatula. Spoon into a decorative bowl or ramekin and store in the refrigerator for up to 1 week.

Muffins
Preheat the oven to 400 degrees. Sift 1 1/2 cups flour, 1/2 cup sugar, the baking powder, baking soda and salt into a large bowl. Toss the peaches with 1 tablespoon flour in a small bowl.

Combine the sour cream, butter, egg and flavorings in a bowl and whisk until smooth. Add to the dry ingredients and mix just until moistened; do not overmix. Fold in the peaches; the batter will be thick.

Spoon the batter into lightly greased muffin cups. Bake for 20 minutes or until puffed and golden brown and a wooden pick inserted into the center comes out clean. Cool in the muffin cups for 5 minutes; remove to a wire rack to cool slightly. Sprinkle with additional sugar and serve warm with the peach butter.

Makes 12

All photography www.tammywingo.com

Applesauce Muffins

1¹/₂ cups all-purpose flour
1 cup sugar
¹/₂ teaspoon baking powder
¹/₂ teaspoon baking soda
1 teaspoon ground allspice
¹/₂ teaspoon nutmeg

¹/₂ teaspoon cinnamon
³/₄ teaspoon salt
¹/₂ cup vegetable oil
¹/₂ cup applesauce
1 egg

Preheat the oven to 350 degrees. Mix the flour, sugar, baking powder, baking soda, allspice, nutmeg, cinnamon and salt in a bowl. Add the oil, applesauce and egg; mix well. Spoon into greased or paper-lined muffin cups. Bake for 15 to 20 minutes or until golden brown. Cool in the muffin cups for 5 minutes; remove to a wire rack to cool completely.

Makes 12

Banana French Toast

4 eggs
2 very ripe bananas, mashed
2 tablespoons milk
2 teaspoons vanilla extract
2 teaspoons cinnamon

3 tablespoons butter
12 slices bread or Texas toast
2 cups sliced bananas, peaches,
    strawberries or other fruit

Preheat the oven to 200 degrees. Combine the eggs, mashed bananas, milk, vanilla and cinnamon in a large shallow bowl; mix well.

Melt ¹/₂ tablespoon of the butter in a 10-inch skillet over medium heat. Dip one slice of bread at a time into the egg mixture, coating both sides. Add to the skillet and cook for 2 to 3 minutes on each side or until golden brown. Remove to a plate and keep warm in the oven. Repeat with the remaining bread slices, adding the remaining butter to the skillet as needed.

Add the sliced bananas to the same skillet used for the toast and sauté until tender. Place three slices of the French toast on each serving plate and top with ¹/₂ cup of the sautéed fruit.

Serves 4

Photograph for this recipe appears on page 50.

Old-Fashioned Stollen (German Coffee Cake)

Old-Fashioned Stollen

2/3 cup milk
1/2 cup sugar
6 tablespoons shortening
1 1/4 teaspoons salt
2/3 cup lukewarm water
2 tablespoons sugar
2 envelopes dry yeast
3 eggs
6 cups all-purpose flour, sifted

Butter for spreading
1/2 cup sugar
1 teaspoon cinnamon
1 (10-ounce) bottle maraschino
    cherries, drained and chopped

Stollen Icing

3 cups confectioners' sugar
3 tablespoons milk
1 1/2 teaspoons vanilla extract

Stollen

Bring the milk just to a low boil in a saucepan and remove from the heat. Stir in 1/2 cup sugar, the shortening and salt. Cool to lukewarm. Mix the water, 2 tablespoons sugar and the yeast in a mixing bowl. Add the milk mixture and mix well. Stir in the eggs. Add the flour and mix to form a dough.

Preheat the oven to 100 degrees. Knead the dough with a dough hook until smooth. Place in a greased bowl, turning to coat the surface; cover with plastic wrap. Place in the oven and let rise for 1 hour or until doubled in bulk. Knead with a dough hook for 3 minutes.

Divide the dough into two portions. Roll each portion into a 12×27-inch rectangle on a lightly floured surface. Spread each with butter. Sprinkle with a mixture of 1/2 cup sugar and 1 teaspoon cinnamon. Sprinkle with the maraschino cherries. Roll the rectangles from the long sides to enclose the filling. Shape into circles and press the ends to seal. Cut shallow slits in the tops of the stollen. Place in greased round pans. Place in the 100-degree oven again and let rise for 1 hour or until doubled in bulk.

Increase the oven temperature to 350 degrees. Bake the stollen for 12 to 14 minutes or until golden brown. Cool in the pans for 5 minutes. Remove to a wire rack to cool completely. Place on serving plates.

Icing

Combine the confectioners' sugar, milk and vanilla in a bowl and mix until smooth. Drizzle over the stollen.

Makes 2 stollen

Sour Cream Coffee Cake

2 cups sifted all-purpose flour	2 eggs
1 teaspoon baking powder	1 teaspoon vanilla extract
1 teaspoon baking soda	1 cup sour cream
1/2 teaspoon salt	1/2 cup packed brown sugar
1 cup granulated sugar	1/4 cup granulated sugar
1/2 cup (1 stick) butter, softened	1 teaspoon cinnamon

Preheat the oven to 325 degrees. Mix the flour, baking powder, baking soda and salt in a bowl. Combine 1 cup granulated sugar with the butter, eggs and vanilla in a mixing bowl and beat until light and smooth. Add the dry ingredients alternately with the sour cream, mixing well after each addition. Combine the brown sugar with 1/4 cup granulated sugar and the cinnamon in a small bowl. Layer the coffee cake batter and brown sugar mixture one-half at a time in a greased 9×13-inch baking pan or bundt pan. Bake for 30 to 45 minutes or until a cake tester comes out clean.

Serves 8

Savory Cheese Pie

2 slices bacon, turkey bacon or Canadian bacon	2 eggs, or equivalent egg substitute
1/4 cup chopped green onions	1 1/2 cups cottage cheese or fat-free cottage cheese
1 1/2 cups all-purpose flour	4 ounces cream cheese or low-fat cream cheese, softened
1 tablespoon baking powder	2 eggs, or equivalent egg substitute
1/2 teaspoon salt	1 tablespoon lemon juice
1/2 cup (1 stick) butter	Garlic salt and pepper to taste
1 cup milk or skim milk	

Preheat the oven to 325 degrees. Cook the bacon in a skillet until crisp; drain and crumble, reserving the drippings. Add the green onions to the drippings in the skillet and sauté until tender.

Mix the flour, baking powder and salt in a bowl. Cut in the butter with a pastry blender or two knives. Add the milk, two eggs and the sautéed green onions; mix well. Spread half the mixture in an ungreased 9-inch deep-dish pie plate.

Combine the cottage cheese, cream cheese, two eggs, the lemon juice, garlic salt and pepper in a bowl; mix well. Stir in the bacon. Spoon into the prepared pie plate and top with the remaining batter, spreading carefully; the top will not be smooth. Bake for 1 hour or until a knife inserted into the center comes out clean. Cut into wedges to serve.

Serves 8

Sausage and Cheese Crepes

1 pound ground pork sausage
1 small onion, chopped
1 cup (4 ounces) shredded Cheddar
  cheese
3 ounces cream cheese, softened

1/2 teaspoon dried marjoram
10 prepared crepes
1 cup (4 ounces) shredded Cheddar
  cheese
1/4 cup chopped fresh parsley

Preheat the oven to 350 degrees. Brown the sausage with the onion in a skillet, stirring until the sausage is crumbly; drain well and return to the skillet. Add 1 cup Cheddar cheese, the cream cheese and marjoram. Cook until the cheeses melt, stirring to mix well.

Spoon the cheese mixture into the centers of the crepes. Roll the crepes to enclose the filling. Arrange seam side down in a lightly buttered 9×13-inch baking dish. Bake, covered with foil, for 15 minutes. Remove the foil and sprinkle with 1 cup Cheddar cheese and the parsley. Bake for 5 to 10 minutes longer or until the cheese melts.

Serves 10

Sausage Breakfast Casserole with Mushroom Sauce

12 ounces sausage
1 cup chopped onion
10 slices bread, cut into cubes
1 1/2 cups (6 ounces) each
  shredded Swiss cheese and
  sharp Cheddar cheese
12 eggs, lightly beaten
2 1/4 teaspoons milk
1 teaspoon dried sage

1/2 teaspoon each salt and pepper
4 cups crisp rice cereal
1/2 cup (1 stick) butter, melted
1/2 cup (2 ounces) grated
  Parmesan cheese
1 (10-ounce) can cream of
  mushroom soup
1 (10-ounce) soup can water
2 cups sour cream

Brown the sausage with the onion in a skillet, stirring until the sausage is crumbly; drain. Layer half the bread cubes, the sausage, Swiss cheese, Cheddar cheese and remaining bread cubes in a 9×13-inch baking dish sprayed with nonstick cooking spray.

Combine the eggs, milk, sage, salt and pepper in a medium bowl and mix well. Pour over the layers in the baking dish. Chill, covered, in the refrigerator for 8 to 24 hours.

Preheat the oven to 325 degrees. Toss the cereal with the butter in a bowl, coating evenly. Sprinkle over the casserole. Top with the Parmesan cheese. Bake for 60 to 70 minutes or until a knife inserted into the center comes out clean. Cut into squares. Heat the soup, water and sour cream in a saucepan over medium heat, stirring frequently. Serve over or with the casserole squares.

Serves 12

Pecan Praline Bacon

3 tablespoons granulated sugar
1/2 teaspoon brown sugar
1 1/2 teaspoons chili powder

1 pound sliced bacon
1/4 cup finely chopped pecans

Preheat the oven to 425 degrees. Mix the granulated sugar, brown sugar and chili powder together. Arrange the bacon in a single layer on a rack in a broiler pan. Bake on the center oven rack for 10 minutes or just until the bacon begins to turn golden brown. Sprinkle with the sugar mixture and pecans. Bake for 5 minutes longer or until brown and crisp. Drain pecan side up on paper towels.

Serves 6

Cranberry Apple Bake

3 envelopes cinnamon-spice
    instant oatmeal
1/2 cup all-purpose flour
1/2 cup packed brown sugar
3/4 cup chopped pecans
1/2 cup (1 stick) butter, melted

3 cups chopped peeled apples
2 cups fresh cranberries
2 tablespoons all-purpose flour
1 cup granulated sugar
Pecan halves and additional fresh
    cranberries, for garnish

Preheat the oven to 350 degrees. Mix the instant oatmeal, 1/2 cup flour, the brown sugar and chopped pecans in a bowl. Add the butter and mix well.

Combine the apples, 2 cups cranberries and 2 tablespoons flour in a bowl; toss to coat evenly. Add the granulated sugar and mix well. Spoon into a 2-quart baking dish. Spoon the pecan mixture over the top. Bake for 45 minutes. Garnish each serving with pecan halves and additional cranberries.

Serves 6 to 8

Baked Cheese Grits

1 cup uncooked grits
1/2 cup (1 stick) butter
8 ounces Velveeta cheese, cubed

1/8 teaspoon garlic powder
3 eggs, beaten
1/2 cup milk

Preheat the oven to 350 degrees. Prepare the grits using the package directions. Add the butter, cheese and garlic powder and stir to mix well. Stir in the eggs and milk. Spoon into a 9×11-inch baking dish. Bake for 40 minutes.

Serves 8

Baked Oatmeal

3 cups rolled oats
1 cup packed brown sugar
1 cup milk
2 eggs

1/2 cup (1 stick) butter, melted
2 teaspoons baking powder
1 teaspoon salt

Preheat the oven to 350 degrees. Combine the oats, brown sugar, milk, eggs, butter, baking powder and salt in a bowl and mix well. Spoon into a 9×13-inch baking dish. Bake for 30 minutes. Serve with berries, cream, sugar, raisins, cinnamon and other toppings of choice.

Serves 5 to 6

Breakfast Time Banana Spread

1/2 cup (1 stick) butter, softened
1/2 banana, mashed
2 tablespoons brown sugar
1/2 teaspoon cinnamon

1/2 teaspoon vanilla extract
Toasted pecan or walnut pieces
   (optional)

Combine the butter, banana, brown sugar, cinnamon and vanilla in a bowl and mix until smooth. Stir in the pecans. Serve with pancakes, waffles, French toast, muffins or your favorite breakfast breads.

Makes about 1 cup

Soups, Salads & Sandwiches

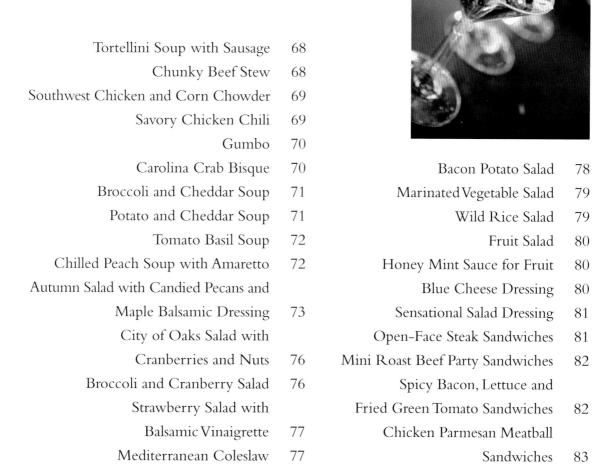

This chapter graciously sponsored by Carolina Woman

Tortellini Soup with Sausage

1 pound sweet Italian sausage links
2 teaspoons olive oil
1 cup coarsely chopped onion
3 garlic cloves, minced
1 pound carrots, sliced
2 (15-ounce) cans diced tomatoes
1 (8-ounce) can tomato sauce
3 (10-ounce) cans beef bouillon, beef
    broth or beef consommé

3 (10-ounce) bouillon cans water
1/2 cup red wine, or 1 cup water
1/2 teaspoon dried basil
1/2 teaspoon dried oregano
3 small zucchini, sliced
1 (7- or 8-ounce) package
    cheese tortellini

Cut each sausage link into eight pieces. Sauté the sausage in the olive oil in a saucepan until brown. Add the onion, garlic, carrots, tomatoes, tomato sauce, bouillon, water, wine, basil and oregano and mix well. Simmer for 30 minutes. Add the zucchini and pasta and simmer for 30 minutes longer.

Serves 8

Chunky Beef Stew

1 small onion, chopped
8 ounces fresh mushrooms, sliced
2 garlic cloves, minced
1 pound lean beef fillet,
    cut into cubes
2 carrots, sliced
2 (16-ounce) cans diced new
    potatoes, drained
1 (16-ounce) can diced tomatoes

1 (28-ounce) can crushed tomatoes
1/4 teaspoon dried oregano
1/8 teaspoon dried thyme
1/4 teaspoon salt
1/8 teaspoon pepper
1 beef bouillon cube
1 cup hot water
Fresh thyme, for garnish

Combine the onion, mushrooms and garlic in a nonstick skillet sprayed with nonstick cooking spray. Sauté over medium-high heat for 5 minutes, stirring occasionally. Combine with the beef in a slow cooker. Add the carrots, potatoes, diced tomatoes, crushed tomatoes, oregano, dried thyme, salt and pepper. Dissolve the bouillon cube in the hot water in a cup. Add to the slow cooker and mix well. Cook on High for 6 hours or longer. Ladle into bowls and garnish with fresh thyme.

Serves 4 to 6

Southwest Chicken and Corn Chowder

2¹/₂ cups chicken broth
¹/₂ cup picante sauce
¹/₂ teaspoon ground cumin
1 (12-ounce) can whole kernel corn
1 small red bell pepper, chopped

1 cup sour cream
2 tablespoons all-purpose flour
2 cups chopped cooked chicken
1 cup (4 ounces) shredded Monterey
   Jack cheese

Combine the broth, picante sauce and cumin in a large saucepan and bring to a boil. Reduce the heat and simmer for 10 minutes. Stir in the undrained corn and bell pepper. Simmer for 5 minutes, stirring occasionally.

Mix the sour cream and flour in a small bowl. Whisk ¹/₄ cup of the soup into the sour cream; stir the sour cream mixture into the soup. Add the chicken and cook until heated through; do not boil. Ladle into bowls and sprinkle with the cheese.

Serves 6 to 8

Savory Chicken Chili

8 large boneless skinless
   chicken breasts
1 cup chopped onion
1 (4-ounce) can chopped green chiles
4 cups chicken broth
5 (15-ounce) cans Great
   Northern beans
1 cup medium or hot chunky salsa
4 teaspoons ground cumin

2 teaspoons garlic powder
2 teaspoons dried parsley flakes
1¹/₂ teaspoons dried oregano
1 teaspoon crushed red pepper flakes
1 tablespoon salt
Shredded Monterey Jack cheese,
   sour cream and tortilla chips,
   for topping

Combine the chicken with enough water to cover in a large Dutch oven. Bring to a boil and cook for 45 minutes or until cooked through; drain. Cut the chicken into bite-size pieces. Combine with the onion, green chiles and broth in the Dutch oven.

Add the beans, salsa, cumin, garlic powder, parsley flakes, oregano, red pepper flakes and salt; mix well. Reduce the heat and simmer for 20 minutes, stirring frequently. Ladle into bowls and top with cheese, sour cream and tortilla chips.

Note: You can freeze the chili, if desired.

Serves 4 to 6

Gumbo

1/2 cup vegetable oil
1/2 cup all-purpose flour
1 cup chopped celery
1 large onion, chopped
1 large green bell pepper, chopped
3 cups chicken broth or chicken stock
1 (16-ounce) can diced tomatoes or
    1 pound fresh tomatoes, chopped
2 cups sliced okra

2 tablespoons chopped parsley
1 to 3 bay leaves
1/2 teaspoon dried thyme
Tabasco sauce and salt to taste
3 cups chopped cooked chicken
1 pound medium to large shrimp,
    peeled and deveined
Hot cooked arborio rice

Heat the oil in a large heavy saucepan. Whisk in the flour. Cook over low heat until dark brown, stirring constantly. Add the celery, onion and bell pepper. Sauté until tender. Add the broth, tomatoes, okra, parsley, bay leaves, thyme, Tabasco sauce and salt; mix well. Simmer for 45 minutes. Stir in the chicken and shrimp. Simmer for 10 minutes longer. Discard the bay leaves and serve the gumbo over rice. You can add sausage, if desired.

Serves 4 to 6

Carolina Crab Bisque

1/2 cup (1 stick) butter
2 cups sliced mushrooms
2 scallions, chopped
1/2 cup chopped onion
1/2 cup chopped green bell pepper
1/4 cup chopped parsley
1/4 cup (1/2 stick) butter
1/4 cup all-purpose flour
4 cups milk

2 chicken bouillon cubes
1/2 teaspoon nutmeg
Tabasco sauce to taste
2 teaspoons salt
1/2 teaspoon pepper
2 cups half-and-half
2 cups crab meat
6 to 8 tablespoons sherry

Melt 1/2 cup butter in a medium skillet. Add the mushrooms, scallions, onion, bell pepper and parsley. Sauté until tender but not brown. Melt 1/4 cup butter in a stockpot and remove from the heat. Stir in the flour. Return to the heat. Add the milk gradually and cook until the mixture thickens, stirring constantly. Stir in the bouillon cubes, nutmeg, Tabasco sauce, salt and pepper. Add the sautéed vegetables and half-and-half. Bring to a boil. Reduce the heat and add the crab meat. Simmer for 5 minutes. Ladle into bowls and top each serving with 1 tablespoon sherry.

Serves 6 to 8

Photograph for this recipe appears on page 66.

Broccoli and Cheddar Soup

3/4 cup (1 1/2 sticks) butter
3/4 cup all-purpose flour
5 1/2 cups half-and-half
1/2 cup heavy cream
6 cups chicken stock or
    chicken bouillon
1 1/2 onions, chopped
1 1/2 teaspoons minced garlic
1 1/2 teaspoons dried thyme

3 tablespoons butter
1 1/2 pounds fresh broccoli florets,
    coarsely chopped
3 cups thin carrot strips
Salt and pepper to taste
1 1/2 pounds sharp Cheddar cheese,
    shredded
1/2 cup dry sherry (optional)

Melt 3/4 cup butter in a large stockpot over medium heat. Add the flour and cook for 3 to 5 minutes to blend well. Cook until the roux is a rich golden brown, stirring constantly. Whisk in the half-and-half, cream and stock. Cook over low heat for 10 to 20 minutes or until thick and creamy, whisking constantly.

Sauté the onions, garlic and thyme in 3 tablespoons butter in a skillet until tender. Add to the soup with the broccoli and carrots. Cook over low heat for 20 to 25 minutes or until the vegetables are tender. Season with salt and pepper. Process one-third of the mixture in a blender or food processor. Return the purée to the soup and add the cheese. Cook until the cheese melts; stir to mix well. Stir in the sherry just before serving.

Serves 12

Potato and Cheddar Soup

3 cups chicken stock
3 cups chopped Yukon Gold potatoes
1 garlic clove, minced
Freshly cracked pepper to taste
1 1/2 cups heavy cream
1/4 cup chopped green onions

2 tablespoons cornstarch
1/4 cup water
2 cups (8 ounces) shredded
    Cheddar cheese
4 slices bacon, crisp-cooked
    and crumbled

Bring the stock to a boil in a saucepan. Add the potatoes. Reduce the heat and add the garlic and pepper. Simmer for 30 minutes. Stir in the cream and green onions. Cook for 15 minutes. Blend the cornstarch and water in a cup. Add to the soup gradually. Bring to a boil and cook until thickened, stirring constantly. Add the cheese and stir until melted. Ladle into bowls and top with the bacon.

Note: You can mash the potatoes with a potato masher before adding the cheese for a smoother texture.

Serves 4

Tomato Basil Soup

1 large onion, chopped
5 tablespoons butter or margarine
3 cups canned tomatoes
1 1/2 tablespoons dried basil
1/2 teaspoon dried thyme leaves
1/2 teaspoon pepper

2 tablespoons all-purpose flour
2 cups chicken broth
1/4 teaspoon baking soda
1/2 teaspoon sugar
1/2 cup half-and-half

Sauté the onion in the butter in a large saucepan for 10 minutes or until tender. Process the tomatoes in a blender until coarsely chopped. Add to the saucepan with the basil, thyme and pepper. Bring to a simmer and cook for 20 minutes.

Whisk the flour with 1/2 cup of the broth in a small bowl until smooth. Add to the saucepan gradually, stirring constantly. Add the remaining 1 1/2 cups broth and cook until slightly thickened, stirring constantly. Simmer, covered, for 25 minutes. Stir in the baking soda, sugar and half-and-half. Heat just until heated through; do not boil.

Serves 4

Chilled Peach Soup with Amaretto

8 fresh peaches, peeled and chopped
2 cups apple juice
1 cup plain yogurt
1/4 cup amaretto

Juice of 1 lemon
2 tablespoons sugar
1/2 teaspoon vanilla extract

Combine the peaches, apple juice, yogurt, amaretto, lemon juice, sugar and vanilla in a blender or food processor. Process until smooth. Chill until serving time.

Serves 8

We may live without friends; we may live without books, but civilized men cannot live without cooks.

Autumn Salad with Candied Pecans and Maple Balsamic Dressing

Candied Pecans
3 tablespoons butter
3 tablespoons brown sugar
3/4 cup pecans

Maple Balsamic Dressing
2 shallots, finely chopped
2 teaspoons Dijon mustard
1 1/2 tablespoons balsamic vinegar
1/2 cup extra-virgin olive oil
1 1/2 tablespoons maple syrup
Salt and freshly ground pepper to taste

Autumn Salad
8 cups torn salad greens, such as
   endive, frisée, radicchio or
   Bibb lettuce
2 red pears, sliced
1/3 cup dried cranberries
1/3 cup shaved Parmesan cheese or
   crumbled goat cheese

Pecans
Melt the butter with the brown sugar in a skillet over medium-high heat, stirring to dissolve the brown sugar completely. Stir in the pecans and toss to coat evenly. Cook for 1 minute. Spoon onto a waxed paper-lined baking sheet to cool, separating with two forks.

Dressing
Combine the shallots, Dijon mustard and vinegar in a large bowl. Whisk in the olive oil gradually. Stir in the maple syrup and season with salt and pepper.

Salad
Add the salad greens, pears and cranberries to the dressing. Toss to coat. Spoon onto serving plates and top with the pecans and cheese.

Serves 6

City of Oaks Salad with Cranberries and Nuts

Honey Mustard Vinaigrette

1 tablespoon honey
1 teaspoon whole grain
    Dijon mustard
1/4 teaspoon each cinnamon, salt and
    freshly ground pepper
1 tablespoon apple cider vinegar
2 tablespoons water
1 tablespoon extra-virgin olive oil

City of Oaks Salad

5 ounces mixed salad greens
3/4 cup dried cranberries
1/4 cup toasted pine nuts, almonds
    or walnuts
1/4 cup (1 ounce) grated Parmesan
    cheese, manchego cheese, blue
    cheese or feta cheese

Vinaigrette

Combine the honey, Dijon mustard, cinnamon, salt and pepper in a small bowl and whisk until smooth. Whisk in the vinegar, water and olive oil.

Salad

Combine the salad greens, cranberries and pine nuts in a large bowl. Add the vinaigrette and toss to coat well. Spoon onto salad plates and top with the Parmesan cheese.

Serves 4

Photograph for this recipe appears on page 66.

Broccoli and Cranberry Salad

6 cups (1-inch) broccoli florets
1 cup (4 ounces) shredded sharp
    Cheddar cheese
1 cup crumbled crisp-cooked bacon
1 cup dried cranberries
1/2 cup chopped red onion

1 cup mayonnaise
2 tablespoons sugar
2 tablespoons red wine vinegar
1/2 teaspoon salt
1/4 teaspoon pepper

Combine the broccoli, cheese, bacon, cranberries and onion in a large bowl and mix well. Combine the mayonnaise, sugar, vinegar, salt and pepper in a small bowl and whisk until smooth. Add to the broccoli mixture and mix to coat evenly. Chill for 1 hour or longer.

Serves 8 to 10

Strawberry Salad with Balsamic Vinaigrette

Balsamic Vinaigrette
1/4 cup vegetable oil
2 tablespoons balsamic vinegar
2 tablespoons sugar
Hot pepper sauce to taste
1/2 teaspoon salt
Pepper to taste

Strawberry Salad
1/3 cup pecans
1 tablespoon butter, melted
2 tablespoons sugar
1 package lettuce
1 pint strawberries, sliced

Vinaigrette

Combine the oil, vinegar, sugar, hot sauce, salt and pepper in a small bowl and whisk until smooth.

Salad

Stir the pecans into the butter in a sauté pan. Sprinkle with the sugar and sauté until the pecans are toasted, stirring to coat well and prevent burning. Spoon onto waxed paper to cool.

Combine the lettuce and strawberries in a bowl. Add the cooled pecans. Add the vinaigrette at serving time and toss to coat evenly.

Serves 6

Mediterranean Coleslaw

1/4 cup extra-virgin olive oil
3 tablespoons apple cider vinegar
2 tablespoons water
1/2 to 1 garlic clove, minced
1/2 teaspoon oregano
3/4 to 1 teaspoon salt

1/2 to 1 teaspoon freshly
    ground pepper
16 ounces coleslaw mix
2 or 3 green onions, chopped
6 ounces feta cheese, crumbled

Combine the olive oil, vinegar, water, garlic, oregano, salt and pepper in a small bowl and whisk to mix well. Combine the cabbage and green onions in a large bowl. Add the dressing mixture and cheese and toss to coat evenly. Chill, covered, for 30 minutes or longer.

Serves 8 to 12

Sultry Summer Shoe Peg Salad

1/2 cup vegetable oil
3/4 cup red wine vinegar
3/4 cup sugar
1 teaspoon salt
1 teaspoon pepper
1 (16-ounce) can Shoe Peg
   corn, drained
1 (16-ounce) package frozen
   cut green beans, thawed
1 (16-ounce) package frozen green
   peas, thawed

1 bunch green onions, chopped
1 red, yellow or orange bell
   pepper, chopped
1 cup chopped celery
1 (4-ounce) jar chopped pimentos,
   drained, or to taste
1 (8-ounce) can water chestnuts,
   drained and chopped

Combine the oil, vinegar, sugar, salt and pepper in a medium saucepan. Bring to a boil, stirring to blend well. Cool to room temperature.

Mix the corn, beans, peas, green onions, bell pepper, celery, pimentos and water chestnuts in a bowl. Add the cooled dressing and toss to coat evenly. Chill until serving time.

Serves 6 to 8

Bacon Potato Salad

6 to 8 russet potatoes, cut into
   1-inch pieces
8 ounces bacon, crisp-cooked and
   crumbled
6 green onions, chopped
2 ribs celery, chopped

3/4 teaspoon salt
1/4 teaspoon pepper
1 cup sour cream or light sour cream
1/2 cup mayonnaise or
   light mayonnaise
Celery sticks and paprika, for garnish

Combine the potatoes with enough water to cover in a saucepan. Bring to a boil and cook for 12 to 15 minutes or until tender. Drain and cool. Combine with the bacon, green onions, chopped celery, salt and pepper in a large bowl.

Mix the sour cream with the mayonnaise in a small bowl. Add to the potato mixture and toss gently to coat well. Chill, covered, for 1 hour or longer. Garnish with celery sticks and paprika.

Serves 6

Marinated Vegetable Salad

1 (17-ounce) can French-style green
    beans, drained
1 (17-ounce) can small green
    peas, drained
1 (16-ounce) can Shoe Peg
    corn, drained
3/4 cup chopped onion
1/2 cup chopped celery

1/2 cup chopped green bell pepper
1 (2-ounce) jar chopped
    pimento, drained
1 cup sugar
3/4 cup vinegar
1/2 cup vegetable oil
1 teaspoon salt
1/2 teaspoon pepper

Combine the beans, peas, corn, onion, celery, bell pepper and pimento in a large bowl. Mix the sugar, vinegar, oil, salt and pepper in a medium saucepan. Bring to a low boil over low heat, stirring to dissolve the sugar completely. Pour over the vegetables and toss gently. Chill, tightly covered, for 12 hours or longer.

Serves 6 to 8

Wild Rice Salad

1 (6-ounce) package long grain and
    wild rice mix
1 cup broccoli florets, chopped
1 cup sweetened dried cranberries
4 green onions, chopped
3 ribs celery, chopped

1/2 red bell pepper, chopped
1/2 cup sweet-and-sour salad dressing
    (tested with Old Dutch sweet-
    and-sour dressing)
1 cup dry-roasted peanuts

Prepare the rice mix using the package directions; cool to room temperature. Combine the rice with the broccoli, cranberries, green onions, celery and bell pepper in a bowl. Add the salad dressing and mix gently. Chill, covered, for 2 hours or longer. Stir in the peanuts at serving time.

Serves 6 to 8

Fruit Salad

4 cups chopped apples
2 cups green grapes
2 cups red grapes
1 (15-ounce) can pineapple
    chunks, drained

1 (15-ounce) can mandarin
    oranges, drained
4 ounces cream cheese
1/2 cup sour cream
1/2 cup sugar

Combine the fruit in a large bowl. Place the cream cheese in a microwave-safe bowl. Microwave on High just until melted. Add the sour cream and sugar and mix until smooth. Add to the fruit and mix gently. Chill until serving time.

Serves 6 to 8

Honey Mint Sauce for Fruit

10 leaves mixed fresh lemon mint
    and spearmint
1/2 cup sourwood honey or
    other honey
1/4 cup light white wine (optional)

Juice of 1 orange
Juice of 1 lemon
Grated orange zest to taste
Grated lemon zest to taste
2 teaspoons poppy seeds

Combine the mint leaves with the honey, wine, orange juice, lemon juice, orange zest, lemon zest and poppy seeds in a blender. Process just until smooth. Serve as a dip for fresh fruit. It is also a good dressing for a fruit salad garnished with fresh mint.

Serves 10 or more

Blue Cheese Dressing

1 cup sour cream
1/2 cup mayonnaise
1 tablespoon apple cider vinegar

8 ounces blue cheese, crumbled
1/4 cup chopped parsley
1 tablespoon minced garlic

Combine the sour cream, mayonnaise and vinegar in a bowl and mix until smooth. Stir in the cheese, parsley and garlic. Chill, covered, in the refrigerator for 2 hours or longer. Serve as a dressing for a lettuce wedge or as a dip for Buffalo wings.

Serves 6

Sensational Salad Dressing

1/2 cup olive oil
1/2 cup vegetable oil
3 tablespoons lemon juice
1/2 cup (4 ounces) grated
   Romano cheese

2 tablespoons parsley flakes
1 tablespoon minced fresh garlic
1 teaspoon oregano
1/2 teaspoon salt
1/2 teaspoon pepper

Combine the olive oil, vegetable oil and lemon juice in a blender. Add the cheese, parsley flakes, garlic, oregano, salt and pepper. Process for 1 minute or until smooth. Store in an airtight container in the refrigerator.

Makes 1 3/4 cups

Open-Face Steak Sandwiches

1 pound flank steak, thinly sliced
1 1/2 cups sliced mushrooms
1/2 cup thinly sliced onion
4 garlic cloves, minced
2 cups beef broth
4 teaspoons cornstarch

3 tablespoons Worcestershire sauce
Dry mustard to taste
1/2 teaspoon each dried thyme, salt
   and pepper
8 slices French bread
Horseradish sauce

Spray a nonstick skillet with nonstick cooking spray and heat over high heat. Add the steak slices and sauté for 2 minutes or until brown. Remove to a plate.

Spray the skillet again and heat over medium heat. Add the mushrooms and onion and sauté for 5 minutes. Add the garlic and sauté for 1 minute longer or until the onion is tender.

Blend the broth with the cornstarch in a small bowl. Add the Worcestershire sauce, dry mustard, thyme, salt and pepper and mix well. Add to the mushroom mixture and cook for 2 minutes or until thickened, stirring constantly. Add the steak and cook for 1 minute longer.

Toast the bread lightly and spread the slices with horseradish sauce. Place two slices on each plate and top with the steak mixture. Serve immediately.

Serves 4

Mini Roast Beef Party Sandwiches

2 (24-count) packages party rolls
1/2 cup whole grain mustard
12 ounces thinly sliced deli roast
    beef, chopped

8 ounces Havarti cheese, thinly sliced
2/3 cup peach preserves

Preheat the oven to 325 degrees. Cut each entire package of rolls into halves horizontally; do not separate the rolls. Spread the mustard on the cut sides of the bottom halves and layer with the roast beef and cheese. Spread the preserves on the cut sides of the top halves of the rolls and place over the filling. Wrap with foil. Bake for 20 to 25 minutes or until heated through. Cut into individual servings.

Serves 12

Spicy Bacon, Lettuce and Fried Green Tomato Sandwiches

2 tablespoons mayonnaise
Worcestershire sauce, lemon juice and
    ketchup to taste
Salt, crushed red pepper and black
    pepper to taste
2 cups all-purpose flour

2 green tomatoes, sliced
1 or 2 eggs, beaten
Vegetable oil for frying
4 slices French bread or other bread
4 to 6 slices bacon, crisp-cooked
Iceberg lettuce or romaine

Combine the mayonnaise with Worcestershire sauce, lemon juice, ketchup, salt, crushed red pepper and black pepper in a small bowl; mix well. Chill in the refrigerator. Combine the flour with red pepper, salt and black pepper in a plastic bag. Soak the tomato slices in the egg in a bowl. Add to the flour mixture and shake to coat well. Fry in the oil in a skillet until golden brown; drain and season with salt. Spread the mayonnaise mixture on half the bread and layer with the tomatoes, bacon, lettuce and remaining bread.

Serves 2

Photograph for this recipe appears on page 66.

Every Southerner knows that tomatoes with eggs, bacon, grits and coffee are perfectly wonderful; that red-eye gravy is also a breakfast food; and that fried green tomatoes are not a breakfast food.

Chicken Parmesan Meatball Sandwiches

2 pounds ground chicken
1 1/3 tablespoons grill seasoning blend
1 egg
2/3 cup Italian-style bread crumbs
1/2 cup chopped parsley
1 or 2 tablespoons extra-virgin
    olive oil
1 1/3 cups grated Parmesan cheese
3 tablespoons extra-virgin olive oil
2 garlic cloves, cut into halves

1/4 teaspoon crushed red pepper flakes
1 teaspoon oregano
1 (16-ounce) can crushed tomatoes
1 cup chicken stock
1/2 teaspoon salt
1 teaspoon pepper
10 fresh basil leaves
8 crusty sub rolls
1 1/2 cups (6 ounces) shredded
    provolone cheese

Preheat the oven to 425 degrees. Mix the chicken with the grill seasoning in a bowl. Mix in the egg, bread crumbs, parsley, 1 or 2 tablespoons olive oil and half the Parmesan cheese. Shape into sixteen flattened meatballs. Place in a baking pan and bake until cooked through. Heat 3 tablespoons olive oil in a medium skillet over medium heat. Add the garlic; sauté for 5 minutes. Discard the garlic. Add the red pepper flakes, oregano and tomatoes. Stir in the stock; season with the salt and pepper. Simmer for 10 minutes; stir in the basil. Add the meatballs and mix gently.

Preheat the broiler. Place the rolls in a baking pan and broil lightly to toast. Spoon the meatballs and sauce onto the roll bottoms, reserving some of the sauce for dipping. Replace the roll tops and sprinkle with the provolone cheese and remaining Parmesan cheese. Broil until the cheese is melted and golden brown.

Serves 8

Grilled Salmon Sandwiches

3 tablespoons brown sugar
2 tablespoons dry mustard
1 1/2 tablespoons water
1 teaspoon olive oil
1/2 teaspoon soy sauce
4 (6-ounce) salmon fillets

2 teaspoons olive oil
Salt and pepper to taste
1/2 bunch arugula
4 slices sourdough bread, crusts
    trimmed and bread toasted

Mix the brown sugar and dry mustard in a small bowl. Stir in the water, 1 teaspoon olive oil and the soy sauce. Preheat the grill. Brush the fish with 2 teaspoons olive oil and season with salt and pepper. Grill until done to taste, turning once. Sauté the arugula in a skillet over medium heat until wilted. Season with salt and pepper. Spoon the arugula and one fillet onto each bread slice on serving plates. Drizzle with the mustard sauce.

Serves 4

Beef & Pork

This chapter graciously sponsored by 18 Seaboard

Spinach Pistou-Stuffed Beef Tenderloin

Spinach Pistou Stuffing

1 bunch parsley
1 cup fresh basil
6 garlic cloves, minced
1 egg
2 tablespoons olive oil
Salt and pepper to taste
2 tablespoons olive oil
1/2 cup chopped onion
1 cup chopped fresh mushrooms
1 cup bread crumbs

1 (10-ounce) package frozen spinach,
   thawed and well drained
1/2 cup (2 ounces) grated
   Parmesan cheese

Spinach Pistou-Stuffed Beef Tenderloin

1 (31/4- to 4-pound) beef tenderloin
11/2 cups dry red wine
11/2 cups low-sodium beef broth
Onion wedges

Stuffing

Preheat the oven to 325 degrees. Combine the parsley, basil, garlic, egg, 2 tablespoons olive oil, salt and pepper in a food processor. Process until puréed. Heat 2 tablespoons olive oil in a small skillet over medium-high heat. Add the onion and mushrooms and sauté until tender. Combine with the puréed mixture in a large bowl. Add the bread crumbs, spinach and cheese; mix well.

Tenderloin

Cut a horizontal pocket in the tenderloin, cutting to but not through the opposite side. Spoon the stuffing evenly into the pocket, leaving the edges clear. Tie the tenderloin with kitchen twine to enclose the stuffing.

Place the tenderloin in a large shallow roasting pan. Pour the wine and broth over the top and arrange onion wedges around the sides. Roast for 40 minutes. Cover tightly with foil and roast for 1 to 11/2 hours longer, basting occasionally. Remove to a cutting board and let stand, covered, for 10 minutes. Remove the twine and cut into 1/2-inch slices.

Note: The longer and slower cooking time in this recipe allows the tenderloin to retain its juices.

Serves 8

Photograph for this recipe appears on page 84.

Perfect-Every-Time Beef Tenderloin

1 tablespoon seasoning salt
1 teaspoon garlic salt
1 teaspoon pepper
1/4 teaspoon dried oregano

1 beef tenderloin, trimmed
3/4 cup red wine
3/4 cup water

Mix the seasoning salt, garlic salt, pepper and oregano together. Rub on all sides of the tenderloin. Place in a roasting pan and cover tightly with foil. Marinate in the refrigerator for 1 hour or longer.

Preheat the oven to 400 degrees. Remove the foil from the roasting pan. Mix the wine and water in a cup and pour into the roasting pan. Roast the tenderloin for 45 to 60 minutes or until done to taste.

Serves 12

German-Style Pot Roast

1 (14-ounce) can beef broth
1 envelope brown gravy mix
1/3 cup cider vinegar
2 tablespoons ketchup
1/4 cup chopped onion

1/2 teaspoon chopped garlic
8 gingersnaps, crushed
1 (2- to 3-pound) boneless chuck
    roast or bottom round roast

Combine the broth and gravy mix in a slow cooker and stir to mix well. Add the vinegar, ketchup, onion, garlic and cookie crumbs; mix well. Add the roast, turning to coat evenly. Cook, covered, on Low for 10 hours or on High for 5 hours. Serve with mashed potatoes.

Note: You can add a small package of baby carrots and 4 chopped red potatoes, if desired.

Serves 4 or 5

Raleigh is one of the few cities in the United States that was planned and built specifically to serve as a state capital.

Great Flank Steak

1 1/2 cups vegetable oil
3/4 cup soy sauce
1/2 cup wine vinegar
1/3 cup fresh lemon juice
1/4 cup Worcestershire sauce
2 garlic cloves, chopped

2 teaspoons dry mustard
1 1/2 teaspoons parsley flakes
2 1/4 teaspoons salt
1 teaspoon freshly ground pepper
1 (2-pound) flank steak

Combine the oil, soy sauce, vinegar, lemon juice, Worcestershire sauce, garlic, dry mustard, parsley flakes, salt and pepper in a bowl and mix well. Combine with the steak in a sealable plastic bag. Seal the bag and marinate in the refrigerator for 8 hours or longer.

Preheat the grill. Drain the steak, discarding the marinade. Grill for 10 to 15 minutes on each side or until done to taste. Cut into thin diagonal slices to serve.

Note: This recipe also works well with a London broil or similar cut of meat.

Serves 4

Whiskey Sauce for One Steak

1 tablespoon butter
8 ounces mushrooms, sliced
2 garlic cloves, chopped

1/2 teaspoon thyme
1/2 teaspoon rosemary
1/2 cup whiskey

Melt the butter in a small saucepan over medium heat. Add the mushrooms, garlic, thyme and rosemary. Sauté for 1 to 2 minutes or until the mushrooms are tender. Remove from the heat and add the whiskey, taking care not to flame. Heat for 1 minute longer, stirring constantly. Serve over steak.

Serves 1 or 2

Spice a dish with love and it pleases every palate.   *—Plautus*

Beef Stroganoff

2 pounds boneless sirloin, cut into
    bite-size pieces
1/2 cup (1 stick) butter
1 1/2 cups chopped mushrooms
1/2 onion, chopped
2 garlic cloves, chopped

2 cups beef stock
1 teaspoon salt
1/2 teaspoon pepper
1/4 cup all-purpose flour
1 1/2 cups sour cream
Buttered hot cooked noodles

Sauté the sirloin in the butter in a skillet until brown on all sides. Add the mushrooms, onion and garlic. Sauté until the vegetables are tender. Stir in the stock, salt and pepper. Simmer for 15 minutes.

Blend the flour with the sour cream in a bowl. Add to the beef mixture and cook until thickened, stirring constantly. Simmer for 15 minutes longer. Serve over hot buttered noodles.

Serves 4

Salisbury Steak

1 1/2 pounds ground beef
1/2 cup cracker crumbs or
    bread crumbs
1 egg
1 small onion, chopped

1/8 teaspoon pepper
1 (10-ounce) can cream of
    mushroom soup
1/3 cup water

Preheat the oven to 350 degrees. Combine the ground beef, cracker crumbs, egg, onion and pepper in a bowl. Add one-fourth of the can of soup and mix well. Shape into six patties. Place in a greased shallow baking dish. Bake for 30 minutes.

Drain the excess drippings from the baking dish. Blend the remaining soup with the water in a bowl. Pour over the patties. Bake for 10 to 15 minutes longer. Serve with mashed potatoes or buttered noodles.

Serves 6

Crescent Lasagna

8 ounces sausage
8 ounces ground beef
3/4 cup chopped onion
1 garlic clove, minced
1 (6-ounce) can tomato paste
1/2 teaspoon each basil and oregano
1 cup cottage cheese
1 egg, beaten

1/4 cup (1 ounce) grated
    Parmesan cheese
2 (8-count) cans refrigerator crescent
    roll dough
2 slices mozzarella cheese
1 tablespoon milk
1 tablespoon sesame seeds

Preheat the oven to 350 degrees. Brown the sausage with the ground beef in a skillet, stirring until crumbly; drain. Mix with the onion, garlic, tomato paste, basil and oregano in a bowl. Mix the cottage cheese, egg and Parmesan cheese in a bowl.

Arrange the roll dough side by side on an ungreased baking sheet, pressing the seams to seal. Layer half the sausage mixture, the cottage cheese mixture and the remaining sausage mixture down the center of the dough. Top with the mozzarella cheese. Fold the edges of the dough over to enclose the filling and press to seal. Brush with the milk and sprinkle with the sesame seeds. Bake for 25 to 30 minutes or until golden brown.

Serves 4 to 6

Barbecue Meat Loaf

1 cup ketchup
1/2 cup water
3 tablespoons apple cider vinegar
2 tablespoons Worcestershire sauce
2 tablespoons sugar
11/2 pounds ground beef
1 cup milk

1/2 cup rolled oats
3 tablespoons chopped onion
11/2 teaspoons salt
1/4 teaspoon pepper
2 slices bacon
2 slices green bell pepper

Mix the ketchup, water, vinegar, Worcestershire sauce and sugar in a bowl. Preheat the oven to 350 degrees. Combine the ground beef, milk, oats, onion, salt and pepper in a bowl and mix well. Shape into a loaf and place in a loaf pan or deep 8×8-inch baking pan. Arrange the bacon and bell pepper over the top.

Bake the meat loaf for 10 minutes. Spoon the ketchup mixture over the top. Bake for 1 hour longer, basting every 20 minutes. Discard the bacon slices before serving.

Serves 6

Mexican Casserole

1 pound ground beef
1 (16-ounce) can chili beans
1/2 cup tomato sauce
2 teaspoons chili powder
1/4 teaspoon garlic powder
1 cup yellow cornmeal
1/2 teaspoon baking soda
1/2 teaspoon salt

1 cup milk
2 eggs, beaten
1 (17-ounce) can cream-style corn
2 cups (8 ounces) shredded
    Cheddar cheese
1 (4-ounce) can chopped green chiles
1/2 cup chopped onion

Preheat the oven to 350 degrees. Brown the ground beef in a large skillet, stirring until crumbly; drain. Add the beans, tomato sauce, chili powder and garlic powder and mix well. Cook until heated through.

Mix the cornmeal, baking soda and salt in a bowl. Add the milk, eggs and corn and mix well. Stir in the cheese, green chiles and onion. Spread half the batter in a greased 9×11-inch baking dish. Top with the ground beef mixture and spread the remaining batter over the top. Bake for 45 minutes or until the topping is golden brown. Let stand at room temperature for 10 minutes before serving.

Serves 6

Frittura Piccata

2 tablespoons all-purpose flour
1/2 teaspoon salt
1/2 teaspoon pepper
1 pound thinly sliced Italian-style veal
    cutlets, cut into 3-inch pieces
1/4 cup (1/2 stick) butter
2 ounces sliced prosciutto,
    cut into slivers

2 tablespoons chicken stock or
    chicken bouillon
1 tablespoon butter
1 teaspoon chopped parsley
2 tablespoons lemon juice
3 or 4 sprigs of parsley, for garnish

Mix the flour with the salt and pepper. Coat the veal with the flour mixture. Melt 1/4 cup butter in a skillet over high heat. Add the veal and sauté for 2 minutes on each side. Remove to a large serving platter.

Add the prosciutto to the skillet and sauté for 3 minutes. Spoon over the veal. Add the stock, 1 tablespoon butter and the chopped parsley to the skillet. Cook for 2 minutes, stirring frequently and scraping up the brown bits. Stir in the lemon juice. Spoon over the veal. Garnish with the parsley sprigs and serve immediately.

Serves 4

Bourbon Street Pork Tenderloin

½ cup peanut oil
¼ cup bourbon
¼ cup soy sauce
¼ cup packed brown sugar
¼ cup Dijon mustard

3 garlic cloves, minced
1 teaspoon Worcestershire sauce
1 teaspoon minced fresh gingerroot,
    or ¼ teaspoon ground ginger
2 (1-pound) pork tenderloins

Combine the peanut oil, bourbon, soy sauce, brown sugar, Dijon mustard, garlic, Worcestershire sauce and gingerroot in a sealable plastic bag. Reserve ⅓ to ½ cup of the mixture. Add the tenderloins to the plastic bag and seal. Place the pork and the reserved marinade in the refrigerator for 8 hours or longer.

Preheat the grill or broiler. Let the pork stand at room temperature for 30 minutes. Drain, discarding the marinade. Grill or broil the pork for 15 to 25 minutes or until cooked through, turning occasionally and basting with the reserved marinade.

Serves 6 to 8

Cranberry Pork Tenderloin

1 (16-ounce) can whole
    cranberry sauce
⅓ cup cranberry juice

¼ cup sugar
⅓ cup golden raisins
2 pounds pork tenderloin

Preheat the oven to 325 degrees. Combine the cranberry sauce, cranberry juice, sugar and raisins in a saucepan. Bring to a boil, stirring to mix well. Pour three-fourths of the mixture over the pork in a 9×13-inch baking dish. Reserve the remaining cranberry mixture in a bowl in the refrigerator.

Bake the pork for 2 hours. Slice the pork and serve with the reserved cranberry mixture.

This is a good dish to prepare in advance for a dinner party. Bake the pork and cool to room temperature; chill in the refrigerator for 8 to 24 hours. Remove from the refrigerator and microwave for several minutes to warm the baking dish. Bake at 325 degrees for 20 minutes to serve.

Serves 6 to 8

You're Invited Back

Pork Tenderloin with Mustard Sauce

Mustard Sauce

1/3 cup mayonnaise

1/3 cup sour cream

1 1/2 teaspoons white vinegar

1 tablespoon dry mustard

Pork Tenderloin

1/3 cup soy sauce

1/3 cup packed light brown sugar

1/4 cup sesame oil

2 tablespoons Worcestershire sauce

2 tablespoons lemon juice

4 garlic cloves, crushed

1 tablespoon dry mustard

1 1/2 teaspoons pepper

1 1/2 to 2 pounds pork tenderloin

Sauce

Combine the mayonnaise, sour cream, vinegar and dry mustard in a bowl and whisk until smooth. Store in the refrigerator.

Tenderloin

Combine the soy sauce, brown sugar, sesame oil, Worcestershire sauce, lemon juice, garlic, dry mustard and pepper in a sealable plastic bag. Add the pork tenderloin; seal and turn to coat evenly. Marinate in the refrigerator for 24 to 48 hours.

Preheat the oven to 450 degrees. Drain the pork, discarding the marinade. Place the pork in a foil-lined 9×11-inch baking pan. Bake for 40 minutes. Let stand for 5 minutes before slicing. Serve with the mustard sauce.

Serves 4 to 6

Southern barbecue is the closest thing we have in the U.S. to Europe's wines and cheeses; drive a hundred miles and the barbecue changes. —John Shelton Reed

Slow-Cooker Barbecue Pork Tenderloin

1 (12-ounce) bottle chili sauce (tested with Heinz)
1 (12-ounce) can cola (tested with Coca-Cola)
3 tablespoons hot pepper sauce (tested with Texas Pete)
2 tablespoons Worcestershire sauce
2 pork tenderloins
1/2 teaspoon garlic powder, or to taste
1/4 teaspoon paprika, or to taste
1/2 teaspoon pepper, or to taste

Combine the chili sauce, cola, hot sauce and Worcestershire sauce in a slow cooker and mix well. Sprinkle the pork with the garlic powder, paprika and pepper. Add to the slow cooker. Cook on Low for 8 hours.

Remove the pork from the sauce and shred with forks. Return the pork to the slow cooker and mix well. Cook until heated through. Serve on rolls as sandwiches.

Serves 6

Asian Glazed Pork Chops

1 tablespoon vegetable oil
4 thick pork chops
1 garlic clove, minced
2 tablespoons vegetable oil
1/4 cup chicken broth or sherry
1/4 cup soy sauce
2 tablespoons brown sugar
1/4 teaspoon crushed red pepper
2 teaspoons cornstarch
2 teaspoons water

Heat 1 tablespoon oil in a skillet and add the pork chops. Cook until brown on both sides. Remove the pork chops to a plate. Add the garlic to the skillet and sauté until tender. Return the pork chops to the skillet.

Combine 2 tablespoons oil with the broth, soy sauce, brown sugar and red pepper in a bowl and mix well. Pour over the pork chops. Simmer, tightly covered, over low heat for 30 to 35 minutes or until the pork chops are cooked through, turning once. Remove the pork chops to a serving platter.

Dissolve the cornstarch in the water in a cup. Add to the cooking liquid in the skillet. Cook until thickened, stirring constantly. Spoon over the pork chops and serve immediately.

Serves 4

Apple Cider Vinegar Pulled Pork

1 (3- to 5-pound) boneless center-cut
   pork roast
1 tablespoon garlic powder, or
   to taste
1 tablespoon salt, or to taste

1 tablespoon pepper, or to taste
2 to 3 cups apple cider vinegar
1 to 2 cups water
1 to 2 cups mustard-based or
   ketchup-based barbecue sauce

Season the pork roast with garlic powder, salt and pepper. Place in a slow cooker. Add the vinegar and water; the liquid should cover only one-half to three-fourths of the roast. Cook on Low for 6 to 8 hours or until the roast is falling apart.

Remove the roast and drain most of the cooking liquid from the slow cooker. Stir the barbecue sauce into the liquid remaining in the cooker. Shred the roast with forks and return to the cooker; mix well.

Serves 6 to 8

Photograph for this recipe appears on page 84.

Cheesy Ham Casseroles

1 (10-ounce) can cream of
   mushroom soup
8 ounces chive and onion-flavored
   cream cheese, softened
2/3 cup milk
8 ounces egg noodles,
   cooked and drained
2 cups chopped baked glazed ham

1 1/2 cups frozen broccoli
   florets, thawed
3/4 cup frozen peas
3/4 cup chopped baby carrots
8 ounces mozzarella, shredded
4 ounces Cheddar cheese, shredded
1/2 sleeve butter crackers, crushed

Preheat the oven to 400 degrees. Combine the soup, cream cheese and milk in a large bowl and mix until smooth. Add the noodles, ham, broccoli, peas and carrots; mix well. Spoon one quarter of the mixture into each of two lightly greased 8×8-inch baking dishes.

Mix the mozzarella cheese and Cheddar cheese in a bowl. Sprinkle half the cheese mixture over the casseroles. Repeat the layers. Sprinkle with the cracker crumbs. Bake for 30 minutes or until light brown and bubbly.

Note: You can wrap one of the casseroles in foil and freeze for later use or to share with a friend. Thaw it in the refrigerator for 8 hours and bake at 400 degrees for 35 to 40 minutes.

Serves 10

Poultry

This chapter graciously sponsored by Urban Food Group

Lemon Chicken with Croutons

Lemon Chicken

1 (4- to 5-pound) roasting chicken
Kosher salt and freshly ground
    pepper to taste
2 lemons, cut into quarters
1 large onion, sliced
Olive oil
2 tablespoons unsalted butter, melted

Croutons

2 tablespoons (or more) olive oil
6 cups (3/4-inch) bread cubes
1/2 teaspoon salt
1/4 teaspoon pepper

Chicken

Preheat the oven to 425 degrees. Rinse the chicken inside and out, reserving the giblets for another use. Trim any excess fat. Sprinkle the cavity with kosher salt and pepper. Place the lemons in the cavity. Tie the legs with kitchen twine and tuck the wings under the body.

Toss the onion with a small amount of olive oil in a small roasting pan. Place the chicken on the onion and pat dry. Brush with the melted butter and sprinkle with kosher salt and pepper. Roast for 1 1/4 to 1 1/2 hours or until the juices run clear when cut between the leg and the thigh; the onion in the pan may burn, but the flavor will be good. Cover with foil and let stand at room temperature for 15 minutes.

Croutons

Heat the olive oil in a large sauté pan until very hot. Reduce the heat to medium and add the bread cubes. Sauté for 8 to 10 minutes or until brown, tossing frequently and adding additional olive oil as needed. Sprinkle with the salt and pepper. Spoon onto a serving platter.

To serve, slice the chicken and place on the croutons. Spoon the pan juices over the top and sprinkle with additional salt. Serve warm.

Serves 3 or 4

Let my words today be sweet and tender, for tomorrow I may have to eat them. —Anonymous

Capital City Chicken

Fresh Tomato Topping

$^2/_3$ pint cherry tomatoes,
   cut into halves
2 tablespoons olive oil
2 tablespoons red wine vinegar
$1^1/_2$ garlic cloves, minced
$^1/_4$ cup chopped fresh basil
Salt and pepper to taste

Capital City Chicken

4 boneless skinless chicken breasts
8 ounces cream cheese or low-fat
   cream cheese, softened
$2^1/_2$ garlic cloves, minced
$^1/_3$ cup sun-dried tomatoes (do not
   use oil-packed)
Salt and pepper to taste
$^1/_4$ cup chopped fresh basil
$^1/_2$ cup (2 ounces) shredded
   Parmesan cheese

Topping

Combine the cherry tomatoes, olive oil, vinegar, garlic, basil, salt and pepper in a small bowl; toss to coat evenly.

Chicken

Preheat the oven to 350 degrees. Pound the chicken to a thickness of $^1/_4$ inch with a meat mallet.

Combine the cream cheese, garlic, sun-dried tomatoes, salt and pepper in a bowl; mix well. Spread the mixture over the chicken, leaving $^1/_4$-inch edges. Sprinkle with the basil and half the Parmesan cheese. Roll the chicken to enclose the filling.

Arrange the chicken seam side down in a greased 9×13-inch baking dish. Sprinkle with the remaining Parmesan cheese, salt and pepper. Bake for 30 to 45 minutes or until the chicken is cooked through. Let stand at room temperature for 5 to 10 minutes before serving. Spoon the tomato topping over the chicken. Serve with saffron rice and a green vegetable.

Serves 4

Chicken with Mushrooms and Sun-Dried Tomatoes

4 boneless skinless chicken breasts
Salt and pepper to taste
1/2 cup all-purpose flour
2 tablespoons butter, softened
1/2 cup chicken broth
1/2 cup dry white wine

1 tablespoon Dijon mustard
8 ounces sliced mushrooms
5 (or more) sun-dried
   tomatoes, chopped
1 garlic clove, minced
1/3 cup sour cream (optional)

Season the chicken with salt and pepper and coat with the flour, shaking off any excess. Heat the butter in a large skillet over medium-high heat. Add the chicken and cook for 3 minutes on each side or until brown.

Add the broth and wine to the skillet and stir up the brown bits. Stir in the Dijon mustard. Cook, covered, for several minutes. Add the mushrooms, sun-dried tomatoes and garlic. Cook, covered, for 5 to 10 minutes longer or until the mushrooms are tender and the chicken is cooked through. Cook longer if needed to reduce the liquid to the desired consistency.

Remove the skillet from the heat and remove the chicken to a platter. Stir the sour cream into the liquid in the skillet and season with salt. Spoon over the chicken.

Serves 4

Chicken Bundles

1 cup bread crumbs
2/3 cup grated Parmesan cheese
1/4 cup fresh parsley, minced
1 teaspoon salt
1/4 teaspoon pepper

3/4 cup (1 1/2 sticks) butter
2 garlic cloves, crushed
8 boneless skinless chicken breasts
Juice of 2 lemons
4 dashes of paprika

Preheat the oven to 350 degrees. Mix the bread crumbs, cheese, parsley, salt and pepper in a medium bowl. Melt the butter in a small saucepan and stir in the garlic.

Pound the chicken breasts with a meat mallet to flatten. Dip into the garlic butter and coat with the bread crumb mixture. Roll the chicken and secure with wooden picks.

Arrange the chicken seam side down in a greased 9×13-inch baking dish. Drizzle with the lemon juice and sprinkle with the paprika. Bake for 1 hour or until crisp and cooked through.

Serves 6 to 8

Pimento Cheese–Stuffed Fried Chicken

Pimento Cheese

12 ounces cream cheese, softened
1 (12-ounce) jar chopped roasted red
    pimentos, drained
1/2 tablespoon mayonnaise (tested
    with Duke's)
1/2 tablespoon hot pepper sauce
    (tested with Texas Pete)
White pepper to taste
8 ounces sharp Cheddar cheese,
    shredded

Stuffed Fried Chicken

4 thick (14-ounce) boneless skinless
    chicken breasts
4 eggs, beaten
1 cup Parmesan bread crumbs (tested
    with Progresso)
1 1/2 cups peanut oil

Pimento Cheese

Combine the cream cheese, pimentos, mayonnaise, hot sauce and white pepper in a food processor. Process until smooth. Add the Cheddar cheese and process just until mixed; the Cheddar cheese should remain in shreds. Chill in a covered container in the refrigerator to thicken.

Chicken

Preheat the oven to 350 degrees. Pound the chicken slightly, leaving it thick enough to stuff. Dip into the eggs and coat with the bread crumbs. Heat the peanut oil in a large skillet until a test bread crumb sizzles when dropped into the oil. Add the chicken to the skillet and fry for 7 minutes. Turn the chicken and fry for 5 minutes longer, taking care to preserve the coating.

Drain the chicken on paper towels and let cool enough to handle easily. Cut a pocket lengthwise down each piece of chicken. Spoon as much pimento cheese as possible into the pockets.

Arrange the chicken in a 9×13-inch baking dish sprayed with nonstick cooking spray. Dollop additional pimento cheese onto the chicken, if desired. Bake for 10 minutes or until the cheese is melted to the desired consistency. Serve hot.

Note: You can double the pimento cheese recipe for more delicious leftovers for sandwiches and snacks.

Serves 4

Riesling Chicken with Grapes

4 boneless skinless chicken breasts
Salt and freshly ground pepper
    to taste
1 tablespoon butter
1 tablespoon vegetable oil
3 tablespoons butter
8 ounces sliced mushrooms
2 leeks, white and pale green
    portions only, finely chopped
1 large shallot, minced
1 garlic clove, minced

1/4 teaspoon salt
1 1/4 cups riesling
2 teaspoons chopped fresh thyme, or
    1/8 teaspoon dried thyme
2 tablespoons chopped fresh tarragon,
    or 2 teaspoons dried tarragon
1 1/2 cups chicken broth
1 teaspoon all-purpose flour
1 cup heavy cream
3/4 cup seedless grapes, cut into halves
Buttered hot cooked noodles

Sprinkle the chicken with salt and pepper to taste. Heat 1 tablespoon butter with the oil in a large heavy skillet over medium-high heat. Add the chicken and cook for 5 minutes on each side or until brown. Remove to a platter and cover with foil; keep warm.

Melt 3 tablespoons butter in the skillet and add the mushrooms, leeks, shallot, garlic and 1/4 teaspoon salt. Sauté over medium heat for 5 to 7 minutes or until the leeks are pale golden brown and the liquid has evaporated. Remove to a bowl with a slotted spoon; keep warm.

Add the wine, thyme and tarragon to the skillet, stirring up the brown bits from the skillet. Cook until reduced to 1/4 cup. Add the broth, chicken and mushroom mixture. Simmer for 20 to 30 minutes or until the chicken is cooked through and tender.

Blend the flour with the cream in a small bowl. Stir into the skillet. Cook until the sauce is thickened, stirring constantly. Stir in the grapes at serving time. Serve over buttered noodles.

Serves 4

The carousel in Raleigh's Pullen Park dates from about 1900, making it one of the earliest of its kind still in operation.

Swiss Chicken

6 boneless skinless chicken breasts

3 eggs, beaten

1 cup bread crumbs

Salt and garlic powder to taste

2 to 3 tablespoons butter

4 ounces mushrooms or sautéed red
    bell peppers

3 thin slices deli Swiss cheese or
    Muenster cheese, cut into halves

1/2 cup chicken broth

Juice of 1 lemon

Combine the chicken with the eggs in a bowl, turning to coat well. Let stand in the refrigerator for 1 hour. Preheat the oven to 350 degrees. Season the bread crumbs with salt and garlic powder. Remove the chicken from the eggs and coat with the bread crumbs; tuck in the ends to make square packets. Cook in the butter in a skillet for 5 minutes on each side. Arrange in a 9×13-inch baking dish. Sauté the mushrooms in the drippings in the skillet. Spoon over the chicken and top each piece of chicken with one piece of cheese. Pour the broth into the baking dish. Bake, covered, for 30 to 45 minutes, removing the cover during the last 10 minutes. Drizzle with the lemon juice at serving time.

Serves 6

Tangy Baked Chicken

4 boneless skinless chicken breasts

2 tablespoons poultry seasoning

Salt and pepper to taste

4 slices bacon

3 tablespoons extra-virgin olive oil

1 onion, cut into quarters

2 garlic cloves

2 sprigs of fresh rosemary

1 cup tomato sauce

1/2 cup chicken stock

1/4 cup balsamic vinegar

3 tablespoons brown sugar

1 tablespoon Worcestershire sauce

Hot cooked pasta

Preheat the oven to 350 degrees. Season the chicken with poultry seasoning, salt and pepper. Cook the bacon in an ovenproof skillet until crisp; drain the bacon, reserving the drippings in the skillet. Crumble the bacon. Add the olive oil to the skillet. Add the chicken and cook until brown on both sides.

Place the skillet in the oven and bake for 15 minutes or until the chicken is cooked through. Remove to a platter and keep warm. Process the onion, garlic and rosemary in a food processor until chopped. Add to the drippings in the skillet and sauté until the onion is translucent. Stir in the tomato sauce, stock, vinegar, brown sugar and Worcestershire sauce. Simmer for 10 to 15 minutes. Serve the chicken over pasta and top with the sauce and crumbled bacon.

Serves 4

Lemon Chicken Risotto

1/2 cup chopped sweet onion
1 tablespoon olive oil
1/4 cup chopped shallots
1 tablespoon butter
1 tablespoon minced garlic
1 tablespoon butter
4 cups chicken stock
2 cups uncooked arborio rice
Salt and pepper to taste
4 boneless skinless chicken breasts,
    cut into bite-size pieces

1 cup (4 ounces) grated
    Parmesan cheese
Cajun seasoning to taste
Juice of 1 lemon
1 cup snap peas
1/2 cup heavy cream
1 tablespoon butter
1 lemon, sliced, for garnish

Sauté the onion in the olive oil in a saucepan. Add the shallots and sauté until tender. Add 1 tablespoon butter and sauté for 2 to 3 minutes or until the vegetables are translucent. Add the garlic and 1 tablespoon butter; sauté over low heat for 30 to 60 seconds. Add the stock; simmer for 3 to 5 minutes.

Add the rice and increase the heat to medium. Season with salt and pepper. Cook until the rice is nearly tender, stirring constantly. Add the chicken and some of the cheese. Cook for 5 to 10 minutes or until the rice is tender and the chicken is cooked through, stirring constantly.

Stir in the Cajun seasoning and half the remaining cheese. Add half the lemon juice, the peas and remaining cheese. Adjust the consistency and taste if necessary with additional cheese, stock or lemon juice. Stir in the cream and 1 tablespoon butter. Garnish with sliced lemon and serve warm with asparagus. You must stir this dish constantly while preparing.

Serves 4 to 6

Photograph for this recipe appears on page 99.

Mexican Chicken Lasagna

2 cups cottage cheese
2 eggs, beaten
1 (4-ounce) can chopped green chiles
1/3 cup parsley, chopped
2 tablespoons vegetable oil
1 onion, chopped
1 red or green bell pepper, chopped
2 garlic cloves, minced
2 (10-ounce) cans tomato soup
1 (10-ounce) can enchilada sauce

2 tablespoons chili powder
1 teaspoon ground cumin
1 1/2 teaspoons salt
1/2 teaspoon pepper
1 (16-ounce) package lasagna
   noodles, cooked and drained
4 cups chopped cooked chicken
8 ounces Cheddar cheese, sliced
8 ounces Monterey Jack cheese, sliced
Refried beans (optional)

Mix the cottage cheese, eggs, green chiles and parsley in a bowl. Heat the oil in a large sauté pan and add the onion, bell pepper and garlic. Sauté over medium heat for 5 minutes. Add the soup, enchilada sauce, chili powder, cumin, salt and pepper; mix well. Simmer for 10 minutes or until thickened, stirring frequently.

Layer the lasagna noodles, cottage cheese mixture, sauce, chicken, Cheddar cheese and Monterey Jack cheese one-half at a time in a 9×13-inch baking dish. Cover and chill in the refrigerator for 8 hours or longer.

Preheat the oven to 375 degrees. Bake the lasagna, covered, for 50 minutes or until bubbly. Let stand, uncovered, for 5 minutes before serving.

Note: You can add a layer of refried beans, if desired.

Serves 10

Raleigh was founded in 1792 as North Carolina's capital city. It was named for Sir Walter Raleigh, who attempted to establish the first English colony on the shores of the New World in the 1580s.

Pesto Chicken

4 boneless skinless chicken breasts,
    thinly sliced
Salt and pepper to taste
4 slices prosciutto

8 ounces chive and onion-flavored
    cream cheese, softened
7 ounces prepared pesto
Freshly grated Parmesan cheese
    to taste

Preheat the oven to 350 degrees. Season the chicken with salt and pepper. Layer the chicken slices on the prosciutto slices on a work surface. Spread the chicken with the cream cheese and a thin layer of the pesto. Roll the prosciutto and chicken to enclose the filling. Arrange seam side down in a baking dish. Top with the remaining pesto and Parmesan cheese. Bake for 30 minutes or until the chicken is cooked through.

Serves 8

Malaysian Chicken Pizza

8 ounces chicken, cut into
    bite-size pieces
3/4 cup rice wine vinegar
1/4 cup soy sauce
1/4 cup packed brown sugar
3 tablespoons water
3 tablespoons chunky peanut butter
4 garlic cloves, minced
1/2 tablespoon minced fresh
    gingerroot

1/2 teaspoon crushed dried red
    pepper flakes
1 recipe pizza dough
1/2 cup (2 ounces) shredded
    Swiss cheese
1/2 cup (2 ounces) shredded
    mozzarella cheese
1/4 cup chopped green onions

Preheat the oven to 500 degrees. Place a pizza stone in the oven to heat if available. Sauté the chicken in a skillet sprayed with nonstick cooking spray. Remove to a plate.

Combine the vinegar, soy sauce, brown sugar, water, peanut butter, garlic, gingerroot and red pepper flakes in a bowl and whisk until well mixed. Pour into the skillet. Bring to a boil over medium-high heat. Cook for 6 minutes or until slightly thickened, stirring frequently. Add the chicken and cook for 1 minute.

Roll the pizza dough into a circle on a floured surface. Sprinkle the Swiss cheese and mozzarella cheese over the dough and spread with the chicken mixture. Slide onto the pizza stone or oven rack. Bake for 8 to 12 minutes or until the crust is crisp. Sprinkle with green onions and serve hot.

You can increase the amount of gingerroot and cheese, if desired.

Serves 6

Barbecue Chicken Pizza

2 chicken breasts, cooked and chopped
1 (8-ounce) bottle honey
    barbecue sauce
8 ounces smoked Gouda cheese,
    shredded

1 red onion, sliced
1 prepared pizza crust
1 green onion, chopped

Combine the chicken with the barbecue sauce in a bowl and mix well. Layer half the cheese and the red onion slices on the pizza crust. Spread the chicken mixture over the onion and top with the remaining cheese and green onion. Cut into wedges to serve.

Serves 3 or 4

Almond Chutney Chicken Lettuce Wraps

1 (3-pound) roasted chicken
1 (9-ounce) jar chutney, chopped
    (tested with Major Grey)
1 cup mayonnaise
2 jalapeño chiles, seeded and minced
1 red onion, chopped
Juice of 3 (or more) large lemons
Grated zest of 1 large lemon

Salt and pepper to taste
3 ribs celery, chopped
1 cup almonds, coarsely chopped
Leaves of 1 head Bibb lettuce
1 bunch fresh basil
1 bunch fresh cilantro
4 radishes, thinly sliced
4 cucumbers, thinly sliced

Cut the chicken into bite-size pieces, discarding the skin and bones. Combine the chutney, mayonnaise, jalapeño chiles, onion, lemon juice, lemon zest, salt and pepper in a large bowl and mix well. Stir in the chicken. Adjust the seasonings to taste. Let stand at room temperature for 20 minutes to blend the flavors or chill in the refrigerator for 8 hours or longer.

Mix the celery and almonds into the chicken mixture. Mound on one end of a large platter. Place the lettuce leaves at the other end. Place the basil and cilantro in the center and arrange the radish and cucumber slices next to the herbs.

To serve, place a few herb leaves in each lettuce leaf and top with a spoonful of the chicken mixture. Add radish and cucumber slices and roll the lettuce to enclose the filling.

Serves 4

Seafood

This chapter graciously sponsored by

B & B Catering and Event Planning

Mahimahi with Avocado-Melon Salsa

Avocado-Melon Salsa
1 small avocado, chopped
1 cup (1/3-inch) cubes cantaloupe
1/4 cup chopped red onion
1/3 cup fresh cilantro, chopped
3 tablespoons fresh lime juice
3/4 teaspoon grated lime zest
Salt and pepper to taste

Mahimahi
4 (6-ounce) mahimahi fillets
1 tablespoon extra-virgin olive oil
3 tablespoons Jamaican jerk seasoning
Hot cooked rice

Salsa
Combine the avocado, cantaloupe, onion, cilantro, lime juice and lime zest in a bowl. Season with salt and pepper. Chill until serving time.

Mahimahi
Preheat the grill. Drizzle the fish with the olive oil and season on both sides with the jerk seasoning. Grill the fish for 4 minutes on each side or until flaky and opaque in the center. Serve over rice and top with the salsa.

Serves 4

Grilled Savory Grouper

8 (6-ounce) grouper fillets, or
    other fish
1 teaspoon chopped fresh herbs, such
    as basil and tarragon
Pepper to taste

1/2 bottle marinade
    (tested with Allegro)
1 (10-ounce) jar peach chutney
2 pears, peeled and chopped

Season the fish with the herbs and pepper. Combine with the marinade in a bowl or sealable plastic bag. Marinate in the refrigerator for 3 hours. Combine the chutney with the pears in a small microwave-safe bowl and mix well. Let stand to blend the flavors while the fish marinates.

Preheat the grill. Drain the fish, discarding the marinade. Grill the fish for 5 to 6 minutes on each side for fillets 1 inch thick. Remove to a serving platter or individual serving plates.

Microwave the chutney mixture on High for 2 minutes. Spoon over the fish to serve. Note: You can also bake the fish in the oven if you prefer.

Serves 8

Salmon with Garlic Parmesan Grits

Garlic Parmesan Grits

1/4 cup chicken broth
1 tablespoon butter
1/4 cup minced onion
1 garlic clove, minced
1 teaspoon salt
3 cups chicken broth
1 cup half-and-half
1 cup uncooked grits
1 teaspoon olive oil
2/3 cup sliced mushrooms
Tips of 2/3 bunch asparagus
1/2 cup (2 ounces) grated
    Parmigiano-Reggiano cheese or
    Parmesan cheese

Salmon

4 (6-ounce) salmon fillets,
    about 1 inch thick
1/4 teaspoon dried thyme
1/4 teaspoon dried sage
1/4 teaspoon salt
1/4 teaspoon pepper
2 teaspoons finely chopped
    fresh parsley

Grits

Combine 1/4 cup broth with the butter, onion, garlic and salt in a small saucepan. Bring to a boil. Reduce the heat and simmer for 5 minutes or until the onion is tender. Add 3 cups broth and the half-and-half and bring to a boil. Whisk in the grits gradually. Reduce the heat and simmer, covered, for 10 minutes or until the grits are thick and tender.

Heat the olive oil in a small nonstick skillet over medium heat. Add the mushrooms and sauté for 3 minutes. Add the asparagus tips and sauté for 3 minutes longer or until the mushrooms are golden brown and the asparagus is tender. Add the vegetables and cheese to the grits and mix well. Keep warm.

Salmon

Preheat the broiler. Sprinkle the fish with the thyme, sage, salt and pepper. Place skin side down in a broiler pan sprayed with nonstick cooking spray. Broil for 10 minutes or until the fish flakes easily when tested with a fork. Remove and discard the skin. Spoon the grits onto serving plates and top with the fish. Sprinkle with the parsley to serve.

Serves 4

Seared Snapper with Lime Salsa

Lime Salsa

1/4 cup olive oil
2 tablespoons lime juice
2 teaspoons fish sauce
1/2 teaspoon brown sugar
1 avocado, chopped
Sections of 1 lime, finely chopped
1 small cucumber, chopped
1/2 red onion, finely chopped
2 large red chiles, seeded and very
    thinly sliced
1/2 cup chopped cilantro
Sea salt and freshly ground pepper
    to taste

Seared Snapper

4 (7-ounce) snapper fillets or other
    whitefish fillets with skin
Sea salt
Vegetable oil for searing

Salsa

Combine the olive oil, lime juice, fish sauce and brown sugar in a bowl and mix to dissolve the brown sugar completely. Add the avocado, lime, cucumber, onion, chiles and cilantro; toss to mix well. Season with sea salt and pepper.

Snapper

Preheat the oven to 400 degrees. Rinse the fish and pat dry; season with sea salt. Heat a small amount of oil in a large ovenproof skillet over high heat. Place the fish skin side down in the skillet. Sear for 1 to 2 minutes or until the skin is crisp and golden brown. Turn the fish. Place in the oven and bake for 8 minutes. Remove to serving plates and top with the salsa.

Serves 4

Crab and Lobster Lasagna

6 tablespoons butter

6 tablespoons all-purpose flour

4 cups milk

Nutmeg to taste

Salt and white pepper to taste

8 ounces fresh spinach leaves

8 ounces Parmigiano-Reggiano
   cheese, grated

2 cups ricotta cheese

8 ounces mozzarella cheese, shredded

1 egg

2 teaspoons chopped garlic

12 ounces lump crab meat

Chopped cooked meat of
   1 1/2 pounds lobster

8 ounces fresh pasta sheets

Preheat the oven to 350 degrees. Melt the butter in a saucepan over medium heat. Stir in the flour and cook for 2 minutes. Whisk in the milk 1/2 cup at a time and season with nutmeg, salt and white pepper. Cook for 4 to 6 minutes or until thickened, stirring constantly. Remove from the heat. Stir in the spinach and half the Parmigiano-Reggiano cheese.

Mix the ricotta cheese, mozzarella cheese, egg and garlic in a bowl. Season with salt and white pepper. Combine the crab meat and lobster in a bowl and season with salt and white pepper.

Spread 1 cup of the spinach mixture in a greased 8×8-inch baking pan. Layer one-fourth of the lobster mixture in the prepared pan and sprinkle with one-fourth of the remaining Parmigiano-Reggiano cheese. Add a layer of pasta and one-fourth of the ricotta cheese mixture. Repeat the layers three times. Top with the remaining spinach mixture. Bake for 45 minutes. Let stand for 10 minutes before serving.

Serves 6

The North Carolina State Capitol and North Carolina Executive Mansion are National Historic Landmarks.

Coastal Carolina Crab Cakes

1 pound lump crab meat, cleaned
8 saltine crackers, crushed
1 egg
1 tablespoon mayonnaise
1 teaspoon spicy mustard
1 teaspoon dried parsley
1/2 teaspoon Worcestershire sauce

1 teaspoon crushed red pepper
Old Bay seasoning to taste
1/2 teaspoon salt
Black pepper to taste
1 cup all-purpose flour
1/2 cup (1 stick) butter

Combine the crab meat with the cracker crumbs, egg, mayonnaise, mustard, parsley, Worcestershire sauce, red pepper, Old Bay seasoning, salt and black pepper in a medium bowl. Mix well.

Shape into six cakes. Coat with the flour. Melt the butter in a sauté pan over medium-high heat. Add the crab cakes and cook for 4 minutes on each side or until golden brown.

Serves 6

Crab and Spinach-Stuffed Flounder

1 (10-ounce) package frozen chopped
    spinach, thawed and well drained
4 ounces crab meat, drained
4 teaspoons minced onion

3 tablespoons mayonnaise
2 teaspoons Dijon mustard
1/8 teaspoon pepper
4 (4-ounce) flounder fillets

Preheat the oven to 375 degrees. Combine the spinach, crab meat, onion, mayonnaise, Dijon mustard and pepper in a bowl. Pat the fish dry and spread evenly with the spinach mixture. Roll the fillets from the narrow end to enclose the stuffing.

Place the rolls seam side down in an oiled baking dish. Cover with foil and bake for 13 to 18 minutes or until the fish flakes easily with a fork.

Serves 4

Grilled Oysters on the Half Shell

24 fresh oysters on the half shell
Cajun seasoning to taste
Salt to taste
Fresh lemon juice to taste
1 white onion, finely chopped

1 cup chopped fresh spinach
1 cup (4 ounces) shredded Monterey
Jack cheese with jalapeño chiles
Sliced lemons, for garnish

Preheat the grill. Sprinkle each oyster with Cajun seasoning and salt and drizzle with lemon juice. Top with the onion, spinach and cheese. Place on the grill and grill for 5 minutes or until the oysters are cooked through and the cheese melts. Garnish with sliced lemons.

Serves 4

Seared Sea Scallops with Orange-Basil Sauce

2/3 cup orange juice
2 teaspoons Dijon mustard
1/4 teaspoon dried basil leaves
1 1/2 pounds sea scallops

1 tablespoon olive oil
Salt and pepper to taste
1 tablespoon butter

Combine the orange juice, Dijon mustard and basil in a small bowl and mix well. Pat the scallops dry and combine with the olive oil in a bowl; toss to coat well. Season on both sides with salt and pepper.

Heat a nonstick skillet over high heat. Add the scallops and sear for 2 minutes on each side or until crusted and brown. Remove to a bowl and keep warm.

Stir the orange juice mixture into the skillet and cook for 1 minute or until reduced by one-half. Tilt the skillet to collect the liquid to one side. Add the butter and any accumulated scallop juices. Whisk until smooth. Serve over the scallops.

Serves 4

Photograph for this recipe appears on page 112.

Shrimp Étouffée

2 ribs celery, chopped
1 white onion, chopped
1 bunch green onions, chopped
1/2 bell pepper, chopped
4 garlic cloves, chopped
1/2 cup (1 stick) butter
1/2 cup all-purpose flour

1 (14-ounce) can chicken broth
Tabasco sauce to taste
Salt, cayenne pepper and black
   pepper to taste
1 (8-ounce) can tomato sauce
1 1/2 pounds uncooked shrimp, peeled
   and deveined

Sauté the celery, onion, green onions, bell pepper and garlic in the butter in a saucepan until tender. Stir in the flour and cook for 2 minutes. Increase the heat and whisk in the broth. Cook until thickened, whisking constantly. Reduce the heat and season with Tabasco sauce, salt, cayenne pepper and black pepper.

Stir in the tomato sauce. Simmer for 5 minutes. Add the shrimp and simmer for 10 to 15 minutes longer or until the shrimp are cooked through.

Prepare this dish a day in advance and store in the refrigerator to allow the flavors to blend. It can also be frozen to serve later.

Serves 6

Raleigh is home to three major state museums of art, history and natural science, all of which are free to the public: the North Carolina Museum of Art, the North Carolina Museum of History and the North Carolina Museum of Natural Sciences.

Shrimp Newburg

1/2 green bell pepper, finely chopped
1/2 onion, finely chopped
1/2 cup sliced mushrooms
3 tablespoons butter
3 tablespoons all-purpose flour
1/2 teaspoon salt
1 1/2 cups milk
1 1/2 tablespoons chopped pimento
3 cups uncooked small peeled shrimp

1 egg yolk
1/4 cup cream
2 or 3 tablespoons white wine, or
   to taste
1 tablespoon chopped parsley
1/8 teaspoon Tabasco sauce
Prepared pastry shells or hot
   cooked rice

Sauté the bell pepper, onion and mushrooms in the butter in a saucepan until tender. Stir in the flour and salt and cook for 2 minutes. Add the milk gradually. Cook over low heat until thickened, stirring constantly. Stir in the pimento and shrimp.

Blend the egg yolk and cream in a small bowl. Stir into the shrimp mixture. Cook until heated through; do not allow to boil. Stir in the wine and parsley; season with Tabasco sauce. Serve in pastry shells or over rice.

Serves 6

Island Shrimp

1 tablespoon sesame oil
1 tablespoon minced fresh gingerroot
3 garlic cloves, minced
2 teaspoons curry powder
1/2 jalapeño chile, seeded
   and chopped
2 pounds uncooked shrimp, peeled
   and deveined

1 1/2 cups coconut milk
Salt to taste
1/2 cup chopped roasted cashews
1/2 cup chopped fresh cilantro,
   for garnish

Heat the sesame oil in a large skillet. Add the gingerroot, garlic, curry powder and jalapeño chile and sauté until very fragrant. Pat the shrimp dry and add to the skillet. Sauté for 4 to 5 minutes or until the shrimp turn pink. Stir in the coconut milk and season with salt. Cook for 1 minute. Top with the cashews and garnish with cilantro. Serve with basmati rice or couscous.

Serves 6

Shrimp with Roasted Tomatoes

5 large tomatoes, each cut into
    8 wedges
3 tablespoons olive oil
2 tablespoons minced garlic
3/4 teaspoon kosher salt
3/4 teaspoon pepper

1 1/2 pounds uncooked medium
    shrimp, peeled and deveined
1/2 cup chopped parsley
2 tablespoons lemon juice
1 cup crumbled feta cheese

Preheat the oven to 450 degrees. Place the tomatoes in a large baking dish. Drizzle with the olive oil and sprinkle with the garlic, kosher salt and pepper; toss to coat evenly. Roast on the top oven rack for 20 minutes. Remove from the oven and stir in the shrimp, parsley and lemon juice. Sprinkle with the cheese. Roast for 10 to 15 minutes longer or until the shrimp are cooked through. Serve warm.

Serves 6

Shrimp and Artichoke Supreme

1 1/2 to 2 1/2 pounds peeled
    cooked shrimp
1 (14-ounce) can artichoke hearts,
    drained and cut into quarters
1 onion, chopped, or 4 green onions,
    chopped
6 ounces fresh mushrooms, sliced
1 garlic clove, crushed
3 tablespoons butter
1 (10-ounce) package frozen chopped
    spinach, thawed and well drained,
    or 1 pound fresh spinach

1 (10-ounce) can cream of
    mushroom soup
1/2 cup mayonnaise
1/2 cup (2 ounces) grated
    Parmesan cheese
2 tablespoons dry sherry
1 tablespoon Worcestershire sauce
Salt and pepper to taste
Grated Parmesan cheese
Prepared pastry shells or hot
    cooked rice

Preheat the oven to 375 degrees. Combine the shrimp and artichoke hearts in a 2-quart baking dish. Sauté the onion, mushrooms and garlic in the butter in a skillet. Add the spinach, soup, mayonnaise, 1/2 cup cheese, the sherry, Worcestershire sauce, salt and pepper; mix well. Add to the shrimp mixture and mix gently. Sprinkle with additional cheese. Bake for 20 minutes. Serve in pastry shells or over rice.

Serves 5

You're Invited Back

Company's Coming Shrimp and Grits

Grits

1½ quarts water
2 teaspoons salt
1¼ cups finely ground
    white cornmeal
8 ounces cream cheese, chopped
2 cups (8 ounces) shredded white
    Cheddar cheese
1 cup (4 ounces) grated
    Parmesan cheese
1 teaspoon pepper

Company's Coming Shrimp

2 tablespoons butter
4 ounces prosciutto, julienned
1 pound uncooked shrimp, peeled
    and deveined
1½ cups sliced mushrooms
1 (4-ounce) jar oil-packed sun-dried
    tomatoes, julienned
Salt and pepper to taste
4 teaspoons lemon juice
2 teaspoons minced garlic
1 cup white wine
½ cup chopped green onions
Chopped fresh parsley and additional
    grated Parmesan cheese,
    for garnish

Grits

Bring the water to a boil in a large saucepan and add 2 teaspoons salt. Sift in the cornmeal gradually, whisking constantly to prevent lumping. Bring to a low boil. Reduce the heat and simmer for 10 to 15 minutes or until thick, whisking frequently. Add the cream cheese, Cheddar cheese and Parmesan cheese; season with the pepper. Cook until the cheeses melt, stirring to blend well. Remove from the heat and keep warm.

Shrimp

Melt the butter in a sauté pan over medium-high heat. Add the prosciutto and sauté until crisp. Reduce the heat to medium and add the shrimp. Cook until the shrimp are pink on the bottom; turn. Add the mushrooms and sun-dried tomatoes; season with salt and pepper. Stir in the lemon juice and garlic. Cook until the shrimp are cooked through, stirring constantly. Add the wine and stir up the brown bits from the pan. Cook for 1 minute longer. Stir in the green onions.

Spoon the grits into a soup bowl or pasta bowl and top with the shrimp and cooking juices. Garnish with parsley and additional Parmesan cheese.

Note: This is an easy dish and a crowd-pleaser for a small dinner party. Using finely ground cornmeal ensures you will have a creamier dish. The grits can be prepared in advance and reheated at serving time, adding a small amount of water if necessary. Prepare the ingredients for the shrimp in advance and put the dish together at serving time.

Serves 4 to 6

Pasta

Italian Pasta Bake

1 pound ground beef
1/2 cup chopped onion
3/4 to 1 (16-ounce) jar
    spaghetti sauce
4 ounces cream cheese, softened

1/2 cup sour cream
8 ounces spinach linguini, cooked
Salt and pepper to taste
1 cup (4 ounces) shredded
    Cheddar cheese

Preheat the oven to 350 degrees. Brown the ground beef with the onion in a skillet, stirring until the ground beef is crumbly; drain. Add enough of the spaghetti sauce to coat the ground beef mixture and mix well. Combine the cream cheese and sour cream in a bowl and mix until smooth.

Place the pasta in a greased 8×8-inch or 9×9-inch baking pan. Season with salt and pepper. Spread the cream cheese mixture over the pasta and top with the ground beef mixture. Sprinkle with the Cheddar cheese. Bake for 30 minutes or until bubbly.

Serves 4

Supreme Spaghetti Sauce

12 cups (3 quarts) water
2 (12-ounce) cans tomato paste
1 (15-ounce) can tomato sauce
1 (4-ounce) can sliced black olives
1½ teaspoons salt
1 pound lean ground beef
3 spicy Italian sausage links, sliced

1 onion, chopped
1 green bell pepper, chopped
8 ounces sliced fresh mushrooms
8 garlic cloves, minced
1/2 cup minced fresh parsley
2 tablespoons Italian seasoning

Combine the water, tomato paste, tomato sauce, olives and salt in a large stockpot. Brown the ground beef and sausage in a large nonstick skillet, stirring until the ground beef is crumbly; remove with a slotted spoon and add to the stockpot. Reserve the drippings in the skillet.

Sauté the onion, bell pepper and mushrooms in the drippings for 5 to 7 minutes or until tender. Add the garlic and sauté for 1 to 2 minutes, stirring constantly. Add to the stockpot with the parsley and Italian seasoning; mix well.

Bring the mixture to a boil. Reduce the heat to medium-low and simmer for 2 hours, adding water as needed for the desired consistency.

Note: You can double the recipe and freeze for future use. You can omit the meat for a vegetarian version or substitute fresh herbs such as oregano, basil or chives for the Italian seasoning.

Makes enough for 1 pound pasta

Bucatini all' Amatriciana

2 tablespoons butter
2¹/₂ ounces pancetta, chopped
1 small onion, finely chopped
1 garlic clove, minced
1 (28-ounce) can diced tomatoes
  (tested with San Marzano)

¹/₄ teaspoon (or more) crushed red
  pepper flakes
Salt and black pepper to taste
16 ounces bucatini rigati, cooked
Grated Parmesan cheese or pecorino
  Romano cheese

Melt the butter in a skillet and add the pancetta; sauté until brown. Add the onion and garlic and sauté until golden brown. Add the undrained tomatoes, red pepper flakes, salt and black pepper. Simmer for 10 to 15 minutes or until desired consistency; the sauce will be thin.

Combine with the pasta in a bowl and toss to coat well. Top with grated cheese.

Serves 4

Fettuccini with Prosciutto

1 cup frozen green peas, thawed
1 tablespoon thinly sliced fresh basil
1 tablespoon butter
8 ounces sliced mushrooms
3 tablespoons butter
4 or 5 slices prosciutto, julienned
6 ounces uncooked fettuccini

6 ounces uncooked spinach fettuccini
¹/₃ cup grated Parmigiano-Reggiano
  cheese
Salt and cracked pepper to taste
Additional grated Parmigiano-
  Reggiano cheese, for garnish

Combine the peas and basil with 1 tablespoon butter in a small saucepan and cook until heated through. Sauté the mushrooms in 3 tablespoons butter in a sauté pan until tender. Add to the peas. Add the prosciutto to the mushroom juices in the sauté pan and sauté for several minutes. Add to the saucepan with the peas and mushrooms.

Cook the pasta using the package directions; drain. Combine with the prosciutto mixture and ¹/₃ cup cheese in a serving bowl. Season with salt and cracked pepper and toss to mix well. Garnish with additional cheese. Serve immediately.

Serves 4 to 6

Chicken Cannelloni

Roasted Red Bell Pepper Sauce

2 (7-ounce) jars roasted red bell
    peppers, drained
1 (16-ounce) jar creamy
    Alfredo sauce
3/4 cup (3 ounces) shredded
    Parmesan cheese

Chicken Cannelloni

8 ounces uncooked cannelloni shells
    or manicotti shells
4 cups finely chopped cooked chicken
1 (10-ounce) package frozen chopped
    spinach, thawed and well drained
16 ounces chive and onion-flavored
    cream cheese, softened
1 cup (4 ounces) shredded
    mozzarella cheese
1/2 cup seasoned Italian-style
    bread crumbs
1 tablespoon parsley flakes
3/4 teaspoon garlic salt
1 teaspoon pepper
1 tablespoon chopped fresh basil,
    for garnish

Sauce

Combine the roasted red peppers, Alfredo sauce and cheese in a blender. Process until smooth, scraping the side of the blender occasionally.

Cannelloni

Preheat the oven to 350 degrees. Cook the pasta using the package directions; drain. Split the shells down the long side.

Combine the chicken, spinach, cream cheese, mozzarella cheese, bread crumbs, parsley flakes, garlic salt and pepper in a bowl and mix well. Spoon the mixture into the pasta shells and press the sides together gently.

Arrange the stuffed shells cut side down in two lightly greased 7×11-inch baking dishes. Pour the roasted red pepper sauce over the top. Bake, covered, for 25 to 30 minutes or until heated through. Garnish with the fresh basil.

Serves 6

Gnocchi with Chicken Sausage, Bell Pepper and Fennel

1 (16-ounce) vacuum-packed package
    uncooked gnocchi
2 teaspoons olive oil
12 ounces Italian chicken
    sausage, casings removed
    and sausage sliced
1 teaspoon olive oil
1 cup thinly sliced fennel
1 red bell pepper, thinly sliced

1 small yellow bell pepper,
    thinly sliced
1 Cubanelle pepper or banana
    pepper, thinly sliced
1 cup thinly sliced onion
3/4 cup (3 ounces) freshly grated
    Parmesan cheese
1/4 teaspoon pepper
1/4 cup chopped fresh flat-leaf parsley

Cook the gnocchi using the package directions, omitting the oil and salt; drain in a colander over a bowl. Reserve 1/2 cup of the cooking liquid. Keep the gnocchi warm.

Heat 2 teaspoons olive oil in a large nonstick skillet over medium-high heat and add the sausage. Sauté for 3 minutes or until light brown, stirring frequently. Remove to a bowl with a slotted spoon.

Add 1 teaspoon olive oil to the skillet. Add the fennel, red bell pepper, yellow bell pepper, Cubanelle pepper and onion. Sauté for 13 minutes or until tender, stirring occasionally. Add the sausage, gnocchi, cheese, pepper and reserved cooking liquid; mix well. Cook for 1 minute, stirring constantly to melt the cheese. Remove from the heat and stir in the parsley.

Serves 4

Spicy Sesame Linguini

1/3 cup peanut oil
3 tablespoons soy sauce
3 tablespoons rice wine vinegar
2 teaspoons sesame oil
1 tablespoon grated fresh gingerroot
1 teaspoon sugar

12 ounces egg linguini
Florets of 1 bunch broccoli
1 pound chicken, cooked and
    chopped (optional)
4 green onions, chopped
2 dried spicy chiles, crushed

Mix the peanut oil, soy sauce, vinegar, sesame oil, gingerroot and sugar in a small bowl. Bring a saucepan of water to a boil and add the pasta and broccoli. Cook for 5 minutes or until the linguini is tender; drain. Combine with the chicken, green onions and chiles in a bowl. Add the dressing and toss to coat evenly.

Serves 4 to 6

Linguini with Spicy Shrimp Sauce

1/3 cup olive oil
1 cup chopped onion
1 (28-ounce) can chopped tomatoes
1/4 cup chopped parsley
1/4 cup (1 ounce) shredded
    Parmesan cheese
1 tablespoon minced garlic
1 teaspoon sugar
1 teaspoon salt

1/2 teaspoon red pepper flakes
1/4 teaspoon black pepper
1 pound uncooked medium shrimp,
    peeled and deveined
16 ounces fresh linguini, cooked
    and drained
Additional shredded Parmesan cheese,
    for garnish

Heat the olive oil in a medium saucepan over medium heat. Add the onion and sauté for 5 minutes. Stir in the undrained tomatoes, parsley, 1/4 cup cheese, the garlic, sugar, salt, red pepper flakes and black pepper. Reduce the heat to low and cook for 20 minutes or until thickened, stirring occasionally.

Add the shrimp. Cook for 3 to 5 minutes longer or until the shrimp turn pink. Add to the hot pasta in a bowl and toss to mix well. Garnish with additional cheese. Serve immediately with crusty garlic bread.

Serves 4

Cajun Shrimp Fettuccini

1/4 cup (1/2 stick) butter
1/2 onion, chopped
1/2 cup chopped green onions
1/4 cup peeled, seeded
    chopped tomato
4 fresh mushrooms, chopped
2 garlic cloves, minced
4 teaspoons minced parsley

2 teaspoons Creole seasoning
1/4 cup shrimp stock
12 ounces fettuccini, cooked
1 pound uncooked medium shrimp,
    peeled and deveined
1/2 cup dry white wine
1/4 cup (1/2 stick) butter

Melt 1/4 cup butter in a large saucepan. Add the onion, green onions, tomato, mushrooms, garlic, parsley and Creole seasoning. Sauté for 30 seconds, stirring gently. Stir in the stock. Simmer until the onion is translucent.

Add the pasta, shrimp and wine. Simmer until the shrimp are cooked through and most of the liquid has evaporated. Remove from the heat and add 1/4 cup butter. Mix gently until the butter melts and the sauce is creamy. Serve immediately.

Serves 6

You're Invited Back

Shrimp Pad Thai

Pad Thai Dressing
1 tablespoon canola oil or other
    light oil
1 teaspoon sesame oil
Juice of 2 limes
3 garlic cloves, chopped
2 tablespoons grated fresh gingerroot
1 jalapeño chile or other hot red
    chile, chopped
Sugar, salt and pepper to taste

Shrimp Pad Thai
6 ounces uncooked rice noodles
2 scallions, chopped
4 ounces bean sprouts, drained
    and rinsed
6 ounces cooked shrimp
1/2 cup coarsely chopped peanuts
Chopped cilantro to taste
Lime wedges, for garnish

Combine the canola oil, sesame oil, lime juice, garlic, gingerroot, jalapeño chile, sugar, salt and pepper in a medium bowl; mix well.

Cook the noodles using the package directions; drain and place in a large serving bowl. Top with the scallions and bean sprouts. Add the dressing and shrimp and mix gently. Sprinkle with the peanuts and cilantro. Garnish with lime wedges.

Serves 4

Pasta with Roasted Red Pepper and Pecans

1 cup pecan halves
Olive oil for toasting
Kosher salt to taste
3/4 cup frozen or fresh lima beans
10 to 12 ounces uncooked spaghetti

1 small onion, chopped
1 garlic clove (or more), minced
1/4 to 1/2 cup extra-virgin olive oil
1/2 cup chopped roasted red pepper
Grated Parmesan cheese, for garnish

Preheat the oven to 300 degrees. Toss the pecans with a small amount of olive oil and kosher salt in a bowl. Spread on a baking sheet. Toast for 4 minutes or until golden brown.

Cook the beans using the package directions; drain. Cook the pasta using the package directions; drain. Cut the pasta into short pieces with kitchen scissors; keep warm.

Sauté the onion and garlic in 1/4 to 1/2 cup olive oil in a large skillet until the onion is tender. Add the roasted red pepper and sauté for 2 minutes. Add the pecans and beans; toss to mix well. Remove from the heat and add the pasta; mix well. Garnish with Parmesan cheese. Serve warm as a hearty side dish or light main course.

Serves 6

Penne with Eggplant

2 eggplant, cut into 1-inch cubes, or
    4 Japanese eggplant, cut into
    1-inch cubes
1 pint cherry tomatoes
3 1/2 garlic cloves, minced
1/4 cup olive oil
2 teaspoons red pepper flakes
1 teaspoon salt
1 teaspoon black pepper
1/4 cup pine nuts

16 ounces uncooked whole
    wheat penne
Salt to taste
1/4 cup torn basil leaves
3 tablespoons olive oil
1/2 cup (2 ounces) grated
    Parmesan cheese
Additional grated Parmesan cheese,
    for garnish

Preheat the oven to 400 degrees. Combine the eggplant, cherry tomatoes and garlic in a bowl. Drizzle with 1/4 cup olive oil and sprinkle with the red pepper flakes, 1 teaspoon salt and the black pepper; toss to coat evenly. Spread in an even layer on a baking sheet lined with baking parchment or foil. Place the pine nuts in a small baking dish. Place the vegetables on the center oven rack. Place the pine nuts on the lower oven rack. Roast the pine nuts for 8 minutes or until golden brown. Roast the vegetables for 35 minutes or until all the vegetables are tender and the eggplant is golden brown.

Cook the pasta in boiling salted water in a large saucepan for 8 to 10 minutes or until al dente, stirring occasionally; drain in a colander over a large bowl. Reserve 1 1/2 cups of the cooking liquid. Keep the pasta warm.

Remove the roasted vegetables to a food processor. Add the basil and 3 tablespoons olive oil. Process until puréed. Combine with the pasta in a large bowl and add 1/2 cup cheese. Add the reserved cooking liquid 1/2 cup at a time, using as much as is needed for a creamy consistency, stirring constantly. Adjust the salt. Sprinkle with the pine nuts and garnish with additional cheese.

Serves 4 to 6

The city's founding fathers called Raleigh the "City of Oaks" and dedicated themselves to maintaining the area's wooded tracts and grassy parks.

You're Invited Back

Sage Mushroom Tortellini

1/4 cup (1/2 stick) butter
1/2 cup chopped shallots
12 ounces shiitake mushroom
 caps, sliced
1 1/4 cups dry white wine
3/4 cup whipping cream

1 1/2 tablespoons chopped fresh sage
Salt and pepper to taste
2 packages uncooked mushroom and
 cheese tortellini
Grated Parmesan cheese, for garnish

Melt the butter in a large skillet over medium-high heat. Add the shallots and sauté for 1 minute. Add the mushrooms and sauté until brown. Stir in the wine and cream. Cook until the sauce thickens. Stir in the sage and season with salt and pepper. Toss with the pasta in a bowl and garnish with cheese.

Serves 6

Summer Pasta with Brie

5 tomatoes
1 wheel Brie cheese, rind trimmed
 and cheese chopped
1 garlic clove, minced
1 cup torn or chopped fresh basil

1 cup olive oil
1 tablespoon salt, or to taste
Pepper to taste
16 ounces uncooked spaghetti

Plunge the tomatoes into boiling water just until the skins loosen; place directly in ice water to stop the cooking process. Slip off the skins and chop the tomatoes.

Combine the tomatoes with the cheese, garlic, basil, olive oil, salt and pepper in a large bowl; mix well. Let stand at room temperature for 4 hours or longer to blend the flavors.

Cook the pasta using the package directions; drain. Add to the tomato mixture and toss to mix well. Serve immediately.

Serves 6

Photograph for this recipe appears on page 126.

Vegetables & Sides

This chapter graciously sponsored by

Tammy Wingo Photography

Asparagus with Lime Sauce

3 pounds fresh asparagus
2 cups mayonnaise
2 cups sour cream
1/3 cup fresh lime juice
1 1/2 tablespoons grated lime zest

2 teaspoons horseradish
2 teaspoons Dijon mustard
1 teaspoon salt
Additional grated lime zest,
   for garnish

Trim the asparagus to serve as a finger food. Steam for 3 to 5 minutes or just until tender; drain and place in cold water to stop the cooking process. Wrap in paper towels and chill in the refrigerator until serving time.

Combine the mayonnaise, sour cream, lime juice, 1 1/2 tablespoons lime zest, the horseradish, Dijon mustard and salt in a bowl; mix well. Chill in the refrigerator for 8 hours or longer.

Serve the chilled asparagus with the lime sauce. Garnish with additional lime zest.

Serves 20

Black Bean Pie

2 (15-ounce) cans black
   beans, drained
1 (15-ounce) can Mexicorn, drained
1 green bell pepper, chopped
1 yellow bell pepper, chopped
1 cup medium salsa

1 teaspoon chili powder
1 deep-dish pie shell
2 cups (8 ounces) shredded
   Mexican cheese
1 flour tortilla
1 refrigerator pie pastry

Preheat the oven to 425 degrees. Combine the beans, Mexicorn, green bell pepper, yellow bell pepper, salsa and chili powder in a microwave-safe bowl. Microwave on High for 2 1/2 minutes.

Spread half the bean mixture in the pie shell and sprinkle with half the cheese. Top with the tortilla. Layer the remaining bean mixture and cheese over the tortilla.

Place the pie pastry over the top and seal the edges; prick with a fork. Bake for 45 minutes. Serve with additional salsa and sour cream. You can freeze the pie, if desired.

Serves 8

Green Beans with Garlic and Red Onion

1¹/₂ pounds fresh green
   beans, trimmed
1¹/₂ tablespoons butter
1 red onion, cut into halves and sliced

1 teaspoon thyme
1 teaspoon rosemary
1 tablespoon chopped garlic
Salt and pepper to taste

Cook the beans in enough water to cover in a saucepan for 15 minutes. Melt the butter in a skillet. Add the onion, thyme and rosemary. Sauté over medium to medium-high heat for 10 minutes, stirring frequently. Add the garlic and sauté for 7 to 8 minutes longer or until the onion begins to brown.

Drain the beans, reserving ¹/₄ cup of the cooking liquid. Add the beans and reserved liquid to the skillet. Season with salt and pepper. Cook for 8 minutes. Serve hot.

Serves 4

Simply Southern Green Beans

4 slices bacon
2 (16-ounce) cans cut green
   beans, drained
2 tablespoons red wine vinegar

2 tablespoons Worcestershire sauce
¹/₄ teaspoon mustard
¹/₄ teaspoon sugar or equivalent
   sugar substitute

Cook the bacon in a large saucepan over medium heat until crisp; drain the bacon on paper towels and crumble. Reserve the drippings in the saucepan. Add the beans, vinegar, Worcestershire sauce, mustard and sugar to the saucepan; mix gently, taking care to leave the beans intact.

Bring to a low boil and cook, covered, over medium heat for 30 minutes or longer. Taste and adjust the seasonings if necessary. Sprinkle with the crumbled bacon. You can easily double or triple this recipe.

Serves 6

Braised Carrots

1/4 cup (1/2 stick) butter	2 tablespoons water
2 onions, chopped	1 teaspoon sugar
8 carrots, peeled and sliced	Salt to taste
1/4 inch thick	

Heat the butter in a sauté pan until foamy. Add the onions. Sauté until tender but not brown. Add the carrots, water, sugar and salt; toss to coat evenly. Simmer, tightly covered, over low heat for 20 minutes or until the carrots are tender.

Serves 4

Corn Casserole

1 (16-ounce) can whole kernel	1/2 cup vegetable oil
corn, drained	1/3 cup sugar
1 (16-ounce) can cream-style corn	Salt and pepper to taste
2 eggs	1 (7-ounce) package corn bread mix
1 cup sour cream or reduced-fat	
sour cream	

Preheat the oven to 350 degrees. Combine the whole kernel corn, cream-style corn, eggs, sour cream, oil, sugar, salt and pepper in a large bowl and mix with a wooden spoon. Stir in the corn bread mix.

Spoon the mixture into a greased 9×13-inch baking pan. Bake for 1 hour. Serve with ham or turkey. This dish freezes and reheats well.

Serves 8

Country Collard Greens

1 (8-ounce) ham shank
2 bunches collard greens
1 head savoy cabbage, chopped

1 teaspoon red pepper flakes
Salt, pepper and pepper vinegar
    to taste

Boil the ham shank in water in a stockpot until the meat is very tender. Remove the ham shank and let cool.

Wash the collard greens well. Cut out the center stems and tear the leaves into small pieces. Add to the stockpot and cook until tender. Add the cabbage, red pepper flakes and salt. Cook for 1 hour or until the cabbage is tender.

Drain and finely chop the cabbage and greens. Remove the meat from the ham shank and add to the greens mixture. Serve with pepper vinegar and additional salt and pepper.

Serves 6

Rosemary Potatoes

2 tablespoons margarine
1 pound unpeeled red potatoes,
    cut into 3/4-inch pieces

1 teaspoon dried rosemary
1/2 teaspoon salt
1/4 teaspoon pepper

Preheat the oven to 425 degrees. Place the margarine in a 9×13-inch baking pan and place in the oven until melted. Add the potatoes, rosemary, salt and pepper to the margarine in the baking pan and toss to coat evenly. Roast for 25 to 30 minutes or until the potatoes are tender.

Note: You can use chopped sweet potatoes as a healthy alternative to the red potatoes. Sprinkle with cinnamon and sugar to taste for a kid-friendly version, or season with sea salt and cayenne pepper to taste. Bake as directed.

Serves 6

Southerners can't stand to eat alone. If we're going to cook a mess of greens, we want to eat them with a mess of people.

—Julia Reed

Smashed Potatoes with a Hint of Garlic

2 whole garlic bulbs
1 tablespoon olive oil
4 pounds white potatoes, peeled and
     cut into quarters
Salt to taste
8 ounces cream cheese, softened

1 cup sour cream
1/2 cup (1 stick) butter, softened
1/4 cup milk
3/4 teaspoon salt
1/2 teaspoon pepper
1/4 cup chopped chives, for garnish

Preheat the oven to 350 degrees. Cut off the pointed ends of the garlic bulbs and place each bulb on a sheet of foil. Drizzle with the olive oil and fold the foil to enclose the garlic. Roast for 1 hour; cool to room temperature. Squeeze the garlic cloves from the bulbs.

Cook the potatoes in boiling salted water in a saucepan for 20 to 25 minutes or until tender; drain and place in a large bowl.

Add the roasted garlic, cream cheese, sour cream, butter, milk, 3/4 teaspoon salt and the pepper. Mash until smooth. Garnish with the chives and serve.

Serves 6

Spinach and Feta Pie

1 (10-ounce) package frozen spinach
1 cup crumbled feta cheese
1/4 cup chopped onion
Garlic powder, salt and pepper
     to taste

1/2 cup baking mix
2/3 cup milk
2 eggs

Preheat the oven to 400 degrees. Place the spinach in a microwave-safe bowl. Microwave on High for 7 minutes or until thawed. Drain and press to remove the excess moisture.

Combine the spinach with the cheese and onion in a bowl. Spread in a greased 8- or 9-inch baking pan. Sprinkle with garlic powder, salt and pepper.

Combine the baking mix, milk and eggs in a bowl and mix well. Pour over the spinach mixture. Bake for 30 minutes. Let stand at room temperature for 5 minutes before serving.

Serves 6 to 8

Butternut Squash Casserole

1 butternut squash	Cinnamon and salt to taste
2 tablespoons butter	1/3 cup chopped pecans
2 tablespoons maple syrup	2 tablespoons brown sugar

Peel and seed the squash and cut into 1 1/2-inch pieces. Steam the squash for 15 to 20 minutes or until tender. Cool slightly.

Preheat the oven to 350 degrees. Combine the squash with the butter and maple syrup in a bowl and mash until smooth. Season with cinnamon and salt. Spoon into a buttered 1-quart baking dish.

Combine the pecans and brown sugar in a bowl. Sprinkle over the squash. Bake for 25 to 30 minutes or until golden brown.

Serves 4

Squash Casserole

1 pound yellow squash, sliced	2 eggs, beaten
1 onion, chopped	1 tablespoon sugar
1/3 cup water	1/4 teaspoon soy sauce
1/4 teaspoon salt	1/8 teaspoon pepper
1/2 cup (2 ounces) shredded Cheddar cheese	1/4 cup (1 ounce) shredded Cheddar cheese
1/4 cup fine cracker crumbs or bread crumbs	1/4 cup fine cracker crumbs or bread crumbs
1/4 cup (1/2 stick) butter	1/8 teaspoon paprika

Preheat the oven to 350 degrees. Combine the squash with the onion, water and salt in a saucepan. Cook until tender; drain. Combine with 1/2 cup cheese, 1/4 cup cracker crumbs, 1/4 cup butter, the eggs, sugar, soy sauce and pepper in a bowl; mash until smooth.

Spoon into a greased 1 1/2-quart baking dish. Bake for 20 minutes. Top with 1/4 cup cheese and 1/4 cup cracker crumbs. Sprinkle with the paprika. Bake for 10 to 15 minutes longer or until golden brown. Serve hot.

Serves 4 or 5

Herb-Scalloped Tomatoes

4 cups canned stewed tomatoes
2 cups stuffing mix
1 small onion, chopped
2 tablespoons sugar
1/2 teaspoon nutmeg
1/2 teaspoon oregano

1/4 teaspoon rosemary
1 tablespoon salt
1/4 teaspoon pepper
1/3 cup stuffing mix
1/4 cup (1/2 stick) butter, sliced

Preheat the oven to 375 degrees. Combine the tomatoes with 2 cups stuffing mix in a bowl. Add the onion, sugar, nutmeg, oregano, rosemary, salt and pepper and mix well. Spoon into a 2-quart baking dish. Sprinkle the top with 1/3 cup stuffing mix and dot with the butter. Bake for 45 minutes.

Serves 6 to 8

Monterey Jack Ratatouille

4 slices bacon, cut into 2-inch pieces
1 cup sliced onion
2 cups sliced peeled fresh tomatoes
1/3 cup tomato paste
1/4 cup olive oil
1 teaspoon minced garlic
3 tablespoons all-purpose flour
1 teaspoon thyme or fines herbes

1 1/2 teaspoons salt
1 1/2 pounds eggplant, sliced
8 ounces zucchini, sliced
1 green bell pepper, seeded
   and chopped
12 ounces Monterey Jack
   cheese, sliced

Preheat the oven to 400 degrees. Sauté the bacon in a saucepan until partially cooked. Add the onion and sauté until the onion is tender and the bacon is crisp. Add the tomatoes, tomato paste, olive oil, garlic, flour, thyme and salt; mix well. Spread half the mixture in a 9×13-inch baking dish.

Spread the eggplant, zucchini and bell pepper in the order listed over the tomato mixture. Layer the remaining tomato mixture and cheese one-half at a time over the vegetables. Bake for 50 minutes.

Serves 6

You're Invited Back

Marinated Grilled Vegetables

1/4 cup balsamic vinegar
3 garlic cloves, minced
2 tablespoons Dijon mustard
2 tablespoons olive oil
1/2 teaspoon salt
1 teaspoon freshly ground pepper
2 zucchini, about 1 pound, cut into
   quarters lengthwise

1 red bell pepper, cut into 8 pieces
1 yellow bell pepper, cut into 8 pieces
8 thick slices sweet onion
8 portobello mushroom caps
1/2 cup crumbled feta cheese, or
   to taste

Mix the vinegar, garlic, Dijon mustard, olive oil, salt and pepper in a small bowl. Combine with the zucchini, red bell pepper, yellow bell pepper, onion and mushroom caps in a sealable 1-gallon plastic bag. Marinate at room temperature for 30 to 60 minutes.

Preheat the grill. Drain the vegetables and place on a grill rack or grill pan sprayed with nonstick cooking spray. Grill for 2 1/2 minutes on each side or until the vegetables are tender and brown. Remove to a serving platter and sprinkle with the cheese.

You can use any firm vegetables of your choice in this recipe.

Serves 8

Photograph for this recipe appears on page 138.

Vegetable Casserole

1 (15-ounce) can Shoe Peg
   corn, drained
1 (15-ounce) can French-style green
   beans, drained
1 cup chopped onion
1/2 cup chopped celery
1 cup (4 ounces) shredded
   Cheddar cheese

1 cup sour cream
1 (10-ounce) can cream of
   celery soup
Salt to taste
1 sleeve butter crackers, crushed
1/2 cup (1 stick) butter, melted
1/4 cup slivered almonds

Preheat the oven to 275 degrees. Combine the corn, beans, onion and celery in a bowl. Add the cheese, sour cream, soup and salt; mix well. Spoon into a greased small baking dish. Sprinkle with the cracker crumbs and drizzle with the butter. Top with the almonds and bake for 45 minutes.

Serves 6

Pineapple Soufflé

1/2 cup (1 stick) butter, softened
1 cup sugar
4 eggs

1 (40-ounce) can crushed
    pineapple, drained
5 slices bread, cubed

Preheat the oven to 350 degrees. Cream the butter with the sugar in a mixing bowl until light and fluffy. Stir in the eggs. Fold in the pineapple and bread. Spoon into a greased 3-quart baking dish. Bake for 1 hour.

Note: This dish goes well with ham.

Serves 6 to 8

Orzo with Tomatoes and Feta

Red Wine Vinaigrette
1/4 cup red wine vinegar
2 tablespoons lemon juice
1 teaspoon honey
1/2 cup olive oil
Salt and pepper to taste

Orzo with Tomatoes and Feta
6 cups chicken broth
16 ounces uncooked orzo
2 cups grape tomatoes, cut into halves
7 ounces feta cheese, cut into
    1/2-inch cubes
1 cup chopped fresh basil
1 cup sliced green onions
Salt and pepper to taste
1/2 cup pine nuts, toasted

Vinaigrette

Combine the vinegar, lemon juice and honey in a small bowl and whisk until smooth. Whisk in the olive oil and season with salt and pepper. Store, covered, in the refrigerator for up to 2 days.

Orzo

Bring the broth to a boil in a large saucepan. Stir in the pasta and reduce the heat to medium. Cook, partially covered, until al dente, stirring occasionally; drain. Place in a serving bowl to cool, tossing frequently.

Add the tomatoes, cheese, basil and green onions to the pasta and stir to mix. Add the vinaigrette and toss to coat evenly. Season with salt and pepper; top with the pine nuts at serving time. Serve at room temperature.

Serves 6 to 8

Lemon Rice

1 (14-ounce) can chicken broth
1/2 broth can water
1/4 cup finely chopped onion

2 tablespoons butter
1 cup uncooked rice
1/4 cup lemon juice

Bring the broth and water to a boil in a small saucepan. Sauté the onion in the butter in a medium saucepan. Add the rice and stir to coat well. Stir in the broth mixture and lemon juice. Cook over medium heat until the liquid is absorbed and the rice is tender. Serve warm or cold.

Serves 6 to 8

Mexican Rice Casserole

1 cup chopped onion
1/4 cup (1/2 stick) butter or margarine
4 cups cooked rice
1 (8-ounce) can chopped green chiles

2 cups sour cream
1 cup cottage cheese
2 cups (8 ounces) shredded
   Cheddar cheese

Preheat the oven to 350 degrees. Sauté the onion in the butter in a sauté pan. Combine the onion with the rice, green chiles, sour cream, cottage cheese and half the Cheddar cheese in a large bowl; mix well.

Spoon into a baking dish and top with the remaining Cheddar cheese. Bake until bubbly and heated through.

Note: You can prepare this dish a day or two in advance and bake at serving time.

Serves 8

I like rice. Rice is great if you're hungry and want two thousand of something.   —Mitch Hedberg

Desserts

This chapter graciously sponsored by Saint Mary's School

Marbled Pumpkin Cheesecake

Gingersnap Crust

1³/₄ cups crushed gingersnaps

2 to 2¹/₂ tablespoons butter, melted

Marbled Pumpkin Cheesecake

24 ounces cream cheese, softened

1³/₄ cups sugar

3 tablespoons all-purpose flour

5 eggs

¹/₂ teaspoon vanilla extract

1 (15-ounce) can pumpkin

2 egg yolks

³/₄ teaspoon cinnamon

¹/₈ teaspoon ginger

¹/₈ teaspoon ground allspice

¹/₈ teaspoon freshly grated or
   ground nutmeg

Crust

Mix the cookie crumbs with the butter in a bowl. Press into a springform pan.

Cheesecake

Preheat the oven to 550 degrees. Beat the cream cheese, sugar and flour in a mixing bowl until smooth. Beat in the eggs one at a time. Mix in the vanilla. Remove and reserve 2¹/₂ cups of the mixture in a separate bowl.

Add the pumpkin, egg yolks, cinnamon, ginger, allspice and nutmeg to the creamed mixture remaining in the mixing bowl. Spread half the pumpkin mixture in the prepared crust. Spread half the plain creamed mixture over the pumpkin and top with the remaining pumpkin mixture.

Drizzle the remaining plain mixture over the top without covering the pumpkin mixture completely. Swirl a small spoon gently through the layers in a figure-eight pattern to marbleize; do not touch the crust. Place the springform pan in a larger baking pan.

Bake on the center oven rack for 12 minutes or until puffed. Reduce the oven temperature to 200 degrees. Bake for 30 minutes without opening the oven. Dome a lightly oiled piece of foil over the cheesecake and bake for 1 hour longer or until the center moves slightly when the cheesecake is shaken.

Loosen the top edge of the cheesecake from the springform pan with a knife. Cool in the pan on a wire rack. Chill, loosely covered, for 6 hours or longer.

Serves 6 to 10

Frozen Peppermint Cheesecake

Chocolate Crust
1¹/₂ cups crushed chocolate wafers
¹/₄ cup sugar
¹/₄ cup (¹/₂ stick) butter, melted

Frozen Peppermint Cheesecake
8 ounces cream cheese, softened
1 (14-ounce) can sweetened
    condensed milk

1 cup crushed hard
    peppermint candies
3 drops of red food coloring
2 cups whipping cream, whipped
Additional whipped cream and/or
    crushed peppermint candies,
    for garnish

Crust
Mix the cookie crumbs with the sugar and butter in a bowl. Press over the bottom and 1 inch up the side of a 9-inch springform pan. Chill in the refrigerator.

Cheesecake
Beat the cream cheese at high speed in a mixing bowl until fluffy. Add the condensed milk, 1 cup crushed candy and the food coloring; mix well. Fold in the whipped cream. Spoon into the prepared pan. Freeze, covered, until firm. Garnish with additional whipped cream and/or candies.

Serves 6 to 8

Raleigh is home to six colleges and universities: North Carolina State University, Meredith College, Peace College, Shaw University, St. Augustine's College and Wake Technical Community College.

Apple Torte

Crumble Crust
$^1/_2$ cup (1 stick) butter, softened
$^1/_3$ cup sugar
$^1/_4$ teaspoon vanilla extract
1 cup all-purpose flour
Pinch of salt

Apple Torte
8 ounces cream cheese, softened
$^1/_4$ cup sugar
$^1/_2$ teaspoon vanilla extract
1 egg
2 or 3 apples, sliced
$^1/_3$ cup sugar
$^1/_2$ teaspoon cinnamon

Crust
Cream the butter, sugar and vanilla in a mixing bowl until light and fluffy. Mix in the flour and salt until crumbly. Press into a 9-inch springform pan.

Torte
Preheat the oven to 450 degrees. Beat the cream cheese with $^1/_4$ cup sugar and the vanilla in a mixing bowl until smooth. Beat in the egg. Spread in the prepared pan.

Toss the apples with $^1/_3$ cup sugar and the cinnamon in a bowl. Arrange in a spiral pattern over the cream cheese mixture. Bake for 10 minutes. Reduce the oven temperature to 400 degrees and bake for 25 minutes longer.

Note: When preparing a recipe that calls for apples, try Braeburn, Rome, Golden Delicious or Winesap for a sweet taste; for a tart flavor use Granny Smith, Gala or Cortland apples. Mix two varieties together—one sweet and one tart—for a blend of flavors.

Serves 8

Cappuccino Freeze

$^1/_4$ cup instant coffee granules
$^1/_2$ cup boiling water
1 (14-ounce) can sweetened
   condensed milk
$2^1/_4$ cups cold water

$^1/_2$ to 1 cup Kahlúa
Whipped topping, for garnish
1 cup grated semisweet chocolate,
   for garnish

Whisk the coffee granules into the boiling water in a small bowl. Combine the sweetened condensed milk with the cold water in a wide-mouth freezer container and whisk to blend well. Add the Kahlúa and coffee mixture and mix well. Freeze for 24 hours or longer. Scoop into cups and garnish with whipped topping and grated chocolate.

Serves 10

Panna Cotta

Balsamic Strawberries

1/4 cup good-quality balsamic vinegar
2 1/2 tablespoons superfine sugar
2 tablespoons lemon juice
3 tablespoons julienned mint leaves
1 (16-ounce) package frozen or fresh
    strawberries, cut into halves

Panna Cotta

2 cups heavy cream
4 1/2 tablespoons superfine sugar
1/4 teaspoon vanilla extract
1 envelope plus 1 teaspoon
    unflavored gelatin
9 to 10 ounces fresh strawberries

Strawberries

Combine the vinegar, sugar and lemon juice in a small saucepan. Heat over medium heat, stirring to dissolve the sugar completely. Cool to room temperature. Pour the cooled mixture over the strawberries in a bowl. Add the mint leaves and toss gently. Chill, covered with plastic wrap, for 1 hour or longer.

Panna Cotta

Combine the cream and sugar in a saucepan. Cook over medium heat until the sugar dissolves, stirring constantly. Bring to a boil and stir in the vanilla. Reduce the heat and simmer for 3 minutes.

Sprinkle the gelatin evenly over the hot cream and let stand for 1 minute. Stir into the cream until completely dissolved. Pour into four 1/2-cup molds. Cover with plastic wrap and chill until set. Invert the molds onto serving plates, wrapping the mold with a cloth dipped in hot water to unmold. Spoon the balsamic strawberries over the top. Serve with the fresh strawberries.

Serves 4

Photograph for this recipe appears on page 152.

Banana Pudding

1/2 cup sugar
3 tablespoons all-purpose flour
1/8 teaspoon salt
1 egg
3 egg yolks
2 cups milk

1/2 teaspoon vanilla extract
1 (12-ounce) package vanilla wafers
5 or 6 ripe bananas, sliced
3 egg whites
1/4 cup sugar

Mix 1/2 cup sugar with the flour and salt in a double boiler. Add the egg and egg yolks. Stir in the milk. Cook over boiling water until thickened, stirring constantly. Remove from the heat and stir in the vanilla.

Alternate layers of the pudding, vanilla wafers and bananas in a 1 1/2-quart baking dish until all the ingredients are used, ending with a layer of pudding.

Preheat the oven to 425 degrees. Beat the egg whites in a mixing bowl until frothy. Add 1/4 cup sugar gradually, beating until stiff peaks form. Spread over the pudding. Bake for 5 minutes.

Note: You can create a double boiler by placing a smaller saucepan or metal bowl over a larger saucepan with an inch or two of boiling water in it; do not allow the bottom of the smaller pan to touch the water.

Serves 8

Photograph for this recipe appears on page 166.

Southerners know instinctively that the best gesture of solace for a friend or neighbor who's got trouble is a plate of hot fried chicken and a big bowl of cold potato salad. For a real crisis, they also know to add a large banana puddin'.

The Best Berry Cobbler

2 pints mixed fresh berries,
    such as blackberries, blueberries
    and/or raspberries
2 tablespoons all-purpose flour
2 tablespoons sugar
1 tablespoon lemon juice
1 cup all-purpose flour

1/2 tablespoon baking powder
1/8 teaspoon salt
1 cup sugar
1 cup (2 sticks) butter, softened
1 egg, beaten
1/2 teaspoon vanilla extract

Preheat the oven to 375 degrees. Combine the berries with 2 tablespoons flour, 2 tablespoons sugar and the lemon juice in a bowl; mix gently. Spread in a 9×13-inch baking dish.

Mix 1 cup flour with the baking powder and salt. Combine 1 cup sugar with the butter, egg and vanilla in a mixing bowl and mix until smooth. Add the flour mixture and mix well.

Spread the batter over the fruit. Bake for 30 to 45 minutes or until bubbly and light brown. Serve warm with vanilla ice cream.

Serves 10 to 12

Blueberry Apple Crisp

2 to 3 cups fresh blueberries
3 cups sliced apples
1/2 cup sugar
2 tablespoons amaretto, or
    2 tablespoons orange juice plus
    a few drops of almond extract

1 tablespoon all-purpose flour
1/2 cup packed brown sugar
1/2 cup rolled oats
1/4 cup all-purpose flour
1/4 cup (1/2 stick) butter
1/4 cup chopped walnuts or pecans

Preheat the oven to 375 degrees. Combine the blueberries, apples, sugar, amaretto and 1 tablespoon flour in a bowl and mix gently. Spoon into a 7 1/2×12-inch baking dish.

Mix the brown sugar, oats and 1/4 cup flour in a bowl. Cut in the butter until crumbly. Stir in the walnuts. Sprinkle over the fruit. Bake for 30 to 35 minutes or until bubbly in the center. Serve with ice cream, if desired.

Note: You can substitute undrained frozen blueberries for the fresh blueberries. Allow the berries to thaw at room temperature for 10 to 15 minutes. Increase the baking time to 50 minutes.

Serves 6 to 8

Chocolate Chess Pie with Raspberry Coulis

Raspberry Coulis

8 ounces fresh raspberries or thawed
    frozen raspberries
2 tablespoons confectioners' sugar, or
    to taste
1/2 tablespoon lemon juice, or
    to taste

Chocolate Chess Pie

1 1/2 cups sugar
3 tablespoons baking cocoa
2 eggs
1 (5-ounce) can evaporated milk
1/4 cup (1/2 stick) butter, melted
1 teaspoon vanilla extract
1 unbaked (9-inch) pie shell

Coulis

Combine the raspberries, confectioners' sugar and lemon juice in a blender and process until puréed. Press through a strainer with a spatula to remove the seeds. Spoon into a condiment squeeze bottle.

Pie

Preheat the oven to 350 degrees. Mix the sugar and baking cocoa in a bowl. Combine the eggs, evaporated milk, butter and vanilla in a mixing bowl. Add the cocoa mixture and beat at high speed until the sugar is dissolved and the mixture is lightly frothy.

Spoon the filling into the pie shell. Bake for 45 minutes or until set. Cool for 2 to 3 hours before serving. Drizzle the coulis over the slices to serve.

Serves 8

Photograph for this recipe appears on page 152.

One cannot think well, love well, sleep well, if one has not dined well.   —Virginia Woolf

Chocolate Bourbon Pecan Pie

1 cup (6 ounces) semisweet
    chocolate chips
1¹/2 cups chopped pecans
1 unbaked (9-inch) deep-dish
    pie shell
1 cup dark corn syrup
¹/2 cup granulated sugar

¹/2 cup packed brown sugar
¹/4 cup bourbon or water
4 eggs
¹/4 cup (¹/2 stick) butter, melted
2 teaspoons cornmeal
2 teaspoons vanilla extract
¹/2 teaspoon salt

Preheat the oven to 325 degrees. Mix the chocolate chips and pecans in a bowl. Sprinkle into the pie shell.

Combine the corn syrup, granulated sugar, brown sugar and bourbon in a large saucepan. Bring to a boil over medium heat and cook for 3 minutes, stirring constantly. Remove from the heat.

Whisk the eggs, butter, cornmeal, vanilla and salt in a bowl. Add to the hot mixture gradually, whisking constantly. Spoon into the prepared pie shell. Bake for 55 minutes or until set. Cool before serving.

Serves 10

Coconut Chess Pie

1 refrigerator pie pastry
4 eggs, beaten
1¹/4 cups sugar
¹/2 cup (1 stick) butter, melted
1 tablespoon white vinegar or apple
    cider vinegar

1 teaspoon vanilla extract
¹/2 teaspoon salt
1 cup flaked coconut

Preheat the oven to 325 degrees. Fit the pie pastry into a pie plate or disposable pie pan, trimming and discarding any excess pastry. Combine the eggs, sugar, butter, vinegar, vanilla and salt in a bowl and beat until smooth. Stir in the coconut. Spoon into the pie shell. Bake for 45 to 50 minutes or until set. Cool before serving.

Note: This is a guaranteed hit and a Southern favorite.

Serves 8

Old-Fashioned Blueberry Cake

3 cups all-purpose flour
1 teaspoon baking powder
1 cup (2 sticks) butter, softened
2 cups sugar

5 eggs, beaten
1 teaspoon almond extract
Pinch of salt
1 quart blueberries

Preheat the oven to 375 degrees. Mix the flour and baking powder together. Cream the butter and sugar in a mixing bowl until light and fluffy. Beat in the eggs, almond extract and salt. Add the flour mixture gradually, mixing constantly until smooth. Fold in the blueberries gently; the batter will be thick. Spoon into a greased and floured bundt pan. Bake for 50 minutes or until a knife inserted into the center comes out clean and the top is golden brown. Cool in the pan for 5 minutes; invert onto a wire rack to cool completely.

Serves 12 to 16

Three-Layer Carrot Cake

Three-Layer Carrot Cake

2 cups grated carrots
2 cups sugar
1/2 cup light-tasting olive oil
4 eggs
2 cups sifted all-purpose flour
2 teaspoons baking soda
1 teaspoon cinnamon
1 teaspoon salt
1 (8-ounce) can crushed pineapple

Creamy Frosting

1/2 cup (1 stick) butter, softened
8 ounces cream cheese, softened
1 (1-pound) package
    confectioners' sugar
1 teaspoon vanilla extract
1 cup chopped pecans

Cake

Preheat the oven to 350 degrees. Grease three 8-inch cake pans and line the bottoms with waxed paper. Combine the carrots, sugar and olive oil in a mixing bowl and mix well. Beat in the eggs one at a time. Add the flour, baking soda, cinnamon and salt and mix well. Stir in the undrained pineapple. Spoon into the prepared cake pans. Bake for 25 to 35 minutes. Cool in the pans for 5 minutes. Remove to wire racks to cool completely.

Frosting

Cream the butter and cream cheese in a bowl until light. Add the confectioners' sugar and vanilla and beat until fluffy. Mix in the pecans. Spread between the layers and over the top and side of the cooled cake.

Serves 10

Pineapple Cake with Cream Cheese Frosting

Pineapple Cake
2 cups sugar
2 eggs, lightly beaten
2 cups all-purpose flour
2 teaspoons baking soda
1 cup chopped walnuts
1 (20-ounce) can crushed pineapple

Cream Cheese Frosting
8 ounces cream cheese, softened
1/2 cup (1 stick) butter or
    margarine, softened
2 cups confectioners' sugar
2 tablespoons milk
1 teaspoon vanilla extract

Cake
Preheat the oven to 350 degrees. Add the sugar, eggs, flour, baking soda, walnuts and undrained pineapple in the order listed to a mixing bowl, mixing constantly until well combined.

Spoon into a greased and floured 9×13-inch cake pan. Bake for 35 minutes. Cool slightly on a wire rack.

Frosting
Combine the cream cheese, butter, confectioners' sugar, milk and vanilla in a mixing bowl and mix until smooth. Spread on the warm cake.

Serves 10

The pineapple has been a universal symbol of hospitality and welcome for many centuries. During early Colonial days in the United States, families would set a fresh pineapple in the center of the table as a colorful centerpiece for a festive meal, especially when visitors joined them in celebration. This symbolized the utmost in welcome and hospitality to the visitor, and the fruit would be served as a special dessert after the meal. Often when the visitor spent the night, he was given the bedroom that had pineapples carved on the bedposts or headboard—even if the bedroom belonged to the head of the household.

Decadent Chocolate Kahlúa Cake

1 (2-layer) package chocolate
   cake mix
1 (4-ounce) package chocolate instant
   pudding mix
2 cups sour cream
4 eggs
3/4 cup vegetable oil

1/2 cup Kahlúa
1 cup (6 ounces) semisweet
   chocolate chips
1/2 cup whipping cream
1 cup (6 ounces) semisweet
   chocolate chips

Preheat the oven to 350 degrees. Combine the cake mix, pudding mix, sour cream, eggs, oil and Kahlúa in a mixing bowl and beat until smooth. Stir in 1 cup chocolate chips. Spoon into a greased and floured bundt pan. Bake for 1 hour. Cool in the pan for 5 minutes and invert onto a serving plate to cool completely.

Place the cream in a microwave-safe bowl. Microwave on High for 1 minute. Stir in 1 cup chocolate chips until melted. Drizzle over the cake.

Serves 12

Cinnamon Spice Pound Cake

1 (2-layer) package spice cake mix
1 (4-ounce) package French vanilla
   instant pudding mix
1/2 cup sugar
3/4 cup vegetable oil

3/4 cup water
4 eggs
1 cup sour cream
1 cup cinnamon chips
2 tablespoons confectioners' sugar

Preheat the oven to 350 degrees. Combine the cake mix, pudding mix and sugar in a mixing bowl; beat until smooth. Add the oil, water, eggs and sour cream in the order listed, mixing well after each addition. Fold in the cinnamon chips.

Spoon into a greased and floured 12-cup bundt pan. Bake for 1 hour. Cool in the pan on a wire rack for 10 minutes. Invert onto a serving plate to cool completely. Sprinkle with the confectioners' sugar

Note: For **Chocolate Chip Pound Cake**, substitute yellow cake mix for the spice cake mix, chocolate pudding mix for the French vanilla pudding mix and semisweet chocolate chips for the cinnamon chips.

Serves 12

Classic Southern Pound Cake

3 cups all-purpose flour	3 cups sugar
3/4 teaspoon baking powder	6 eggs, at room temperature
1/4 teaspoon salt	1 cup evaporated milk
1 cup (2 sticks) butter, softened	1 teaspoon lemon extract
1/2 cup shortening	1 teaspoon vanilla extract

Preheat the oven to 325 degrees. Sift the flour, baking powder and salt together. Cream the butter, shortening and sugar in a mixing bowl until light and fluffy. Beat in the eggs one at a time. Add the flour mixture alternately with the evaporated milk, mixing well after each addition. Stir in the flavorings.

Spoon the batter into a greased and floured tube pan. Place on the center oven rack and bake for 1 hour and 20 minutes or until a wooden pick inserted into the center comes out clean. Cool in the pan for 15 minutes. Invert onto a wire rack to cool completely.

Note: Pound cake is a staple at Southern church and family events. It takes its name from the tradition of tossing in a pound of each of the main ingredients, from butter to flour, to make the perfect cake.

Serves 16

Photograph for this recipe appears on page 152.

Rum Cake

1/2 to 1 cup chopped pecans (optional)	1/2 cup vegetable oil
	1/2 cup rum
1 (2-layer) package butter cake mix	1 cup sugar
1 (4-ounce) package vanilla pudding and pie filling mix	1/2 cup (1 stick) butter
	1/4 cup water
4 eggs	1/4 cup rum
1/2 cup water	

Preheat the oven to 325 degrees. Sprinkle the pecans in a greased and floured bundt pan. Combine the cake mix, pudding mix, eggs, 1/2 cup water, the oil and 1/2 cup rum in a mixing bowl and beat until smooth. Spoon into the prepared bundt pan. Bake for 1 hour.

Combine the sugar, butter, 1/4 cup water and 1/4 cup rum in a saucepan. Bring to a boil, stirring to melt the butter and dissolve the sugar. Pour over the warm cake in the bundt pan. Let stand for 10 minutes and invert onto a serving plate.

Serves 8

Wolfpack Red Velvet Cake

Cream Cheese Frosting
16 ounces cream cheese, softened
1 cup (2 sticks) butter, softened
1 teaspoon vanilla extract
4 cups confectioners' sugar, sifted

Wolfpack Red Velvet Cake
2 1/4 cups sifted cake flour
2 tablespoons baking cocoa

1 teaspoon baking soda
1/4 teaspoon salt
1/2 cup (1 stick) butter, softened
4 ounces light cream cheese, softened
1 1/2 cups sugar
2 eggs
2 ounces red food coloring
1 cup buttermilk
1 teaspoon vanilla extract

Frosting
Beat the cream cheese, butter and vanilla in a mixing bowl until creamy. Add the confectioners' sugar gradually, mixing at low to medium speed until light and fluffy. Chill in the refrigerator for ease of spreading.

Cake
Preheat the oven to 350 degrees. Mix the flour, baking cocoa, baking soda and salt together. Beat the butter and cream cheese in a mixing bowl until creamy. Add the sugar gradually, beating until smooth. Beat in the eggs and food coloring. Add the dry ingredients alternately with the buttermilk, mixing well after each addition. Stir in the vanilla.

Spoon the batter into two 9-inch cake pans sprayed with nonstick cooking spray. Bake for 20 to 25 minutes or until the layers test done. Cool in the pans for 10 minutes. Remove to a wire rack to cool completely. Spread the frosting between the layers and over the top and side of the cooled cake.

Note: You can combine 1 cup milk with 1 tablespoon vinegar and let stand for 15 minutes to use as a substitute for buttermilk. To substitute all-purpose flour for cake flour, reduce each cup of flour by 2 tablespoons.

Serves 12

I like the South because of the people. They are loyal. Once they love a team, they're fans forever. —Dominique Wilkins

Lemon Icebox Cake

Lemon Glaze

1/2 cup sugar
1 to 1 1/2 tablespoons cornstarch
1/4 teaspoon salt
1/3 cup lemon juice
1/4 cup water
1 egg yolk
1 tablespoon butter
1 teaspoon grated lemon zest

Lemon Icebox Cake

2 eggs
3/4 cup sugar
Juice of 1 lemon
Juice of 1 orange
2 cups heavy whipping cream
1 prepared round or loaf
   angel food cake

Glaze

Mix the sugar, cornstarch and salt in a heavy saucepan. Combine the lemon juice, water and egg yolk in a small bowl and mix well. Add to the saucepan and mix well. Bring to a boil over low heat and cook until smooth and thickened, stirring constantly. Stir in the butter and lemon zest. Cool to room temperature.

Cake

Combine the eggs, sugar, lemon juice and orange juice in a saucepan and mix well. Bring to a boil over medium heat and cook until the mixture coats the back of a spoon. Cool to room temperature. Chill until thickened.

Beat the whipping cream in a bowl until firm peaks form. Fold in the chilled mixture gently.

Cut the cake horizontally into three layers. Spread the chilled mixture between the layers and over the top and side of the cake. Drizzle with the lemon glaze. Store in the refrigerator.

Serves 8 to 10

Strawberry Cake with Buttercream Frosting

Strawberry Cake

1 3/4 cups sliced fresh strawberries
Sugar to taste
1 (2-layer) package yellow cake mix
1 (3-ounce) package
　　strawberry gelatin
4 eggs
1/4 cup all-purpose flour
1 cup light-tasting olive oil

Buttercream Frosting

1 1/2 cups (3 sticks) unsalted butter,
　　softened
4 cups sifted confectioners' sugar
2 tablespoons milk
1/2 teaspoon almond extract
1/2 teaspoon vanilla extract

Cake

Preheat the oven to 350 degrees. Combine the strawberries with sugar in a bowl and mix well. Let stand for 1 hour. Combine the strawberries and accumulated juices with the cake mix, gelatin, eggs, flour and olive oil in a mixing bowl. Beat until well mixed. Spoon into two buttered and floured 8-inch cake pans. Bake for 40 to 50 minutes. Cool in the pans for 10 minutes. Remove to a wire rack to cool completely.

Frosting

Beat the butter at medium speed in a mixing bowl until light. Add the confectioners' sugar gradually, beating until fluffy. Beat in the milk. Stir in the flavorings. Spread between the layers and over the top and side of the cake.

Serves 12

Raleigh has an exceptionally diverse arts scene and offers four disciplines of performing arts: theater, opera, symphony and ballet.

Cheerwine Cups

Cheerwine Cups

1 (2-layer) package white cake mix
1 (3-ounce) package cherry gelatin
4 eggs
1/2 cup vegetable oil
1 cup Cheerwine soda

Cherry Cream Cheese Frosting

8 ounces cream cheese, softened
1/4 cup (1/2 stick) butter, softened
1 1/2 cups confectioners' sugar
1 1/2 teaspoons cherry extract

Cups

Preheat the oven to 325 degrees. Mix the cake mix and gelatin in a large mixing bowl. Make a well in the center. Add the eggs, oil and Cheerwine soda to the well. Beat at low speed until blended. Increase the speed to medium and beat for 5 minutes or until smooth.

Spoon into greased and floured miniature muffin cups. Bake for 10 to 12 minutes or until golden brown. Cool in the pans for 1 minute. Remove to a wire rack to cool completely.

Frosting

Beat the cream cheese and butter in a mixing bowl until smooth. Add the confectioners' sugar and cherry extract, beating constantly until light and fluffy. Spread over the muffins and decorate as desired.

Makes 75

Pumpkin Squares

1 (2-layer) package yellow cake mix
1/2 cup (1 stick) margarine, melted
3 eggs
1 (15-ounce) can pumpkin
2/3 cup evaporated milk

3/4 cup sugar
4 teaspoons cinnamon
2 tablespoons butter, melted
Whipped cream

Preheat the oven to 400 degrees. Reserve 1 cup of the cake mix. Combine the remaining cake mix with the margarine and 1 of the eggs in a bowl; mix until crumbly. Press over the bottom of a greased and lightly floured 9×12-inch baking pan. Bake for 10 minutes. Reduce the oven temperature to 350 degrees. Combine the pumpkin with the remaining 2 eggs, the evaporated milk, 1/2 cup of the sugar and half the cinnamon in a bowl; mix well. Spoon over the baked layer. Combine the reserved cake mix with the butter and the remaining 1/4 cup sugar and cinnamon in a bowl; mix well. Sprinkle over the filling. Bake for 35 minutes. Cut into squares and serve with whipped cream.

Serves 24

Chocolate Chip Monster Cookies

5 cups rolled oats
4 1/2 cups all-purpose flour
2 teaspoons baking powder
2 teaspoons baking soda
1 teaspoon salt
2 cups (4 sticks) butter, softened
2 cups granulated sugar
2 cups packed dark brown sugar
3 tablespoons molasses

1 tablespoon honey
1/4 teaspoon salt
4 eggs
2 1/2 teaspoons vanilla extract
4 cups (24 ounces) semisweet
   chocolate chips
1 (8-ounce) chocolate bar, grated
2 1/2 cups chopped nuts (optional)

Preheat the oven to 375 degrees. Process the oats to a fine powder in batches in a food processor or blender. Mix with the flour, baking powder, baking soda and 1 teaspoon salt in a bowl.

Cream the butter with the granulated sugar, brown sugar, molasses, honey and 1/4 teaspoon salt in a mixing bowl. Beat in the eggs and vanilla. Add the dry ingredients in five batches, mixing well after each addition. Stir in the chocolate chips, grated chocolate and nuts.

Shape into uniform balls with an ice cream scoop or by hand and place on cookie sheets lined with baking parchment. Bake for 11 to 13 minutes or until golden brown. Cool on the cookie sheets for 5 minutes. Remove to a wire rack to cool completely.

Note: The molasses and honey in this recipe add depth of flavor and moistness to the cookies.

Makes 45 large or 85 small cookies

Chocolate Crinkles

4 eggs
2 cups sugar
2 cups all-purpose flour
1 cup baking cocoa
1/2 cup vegetable oil

2 teaspoons baking powder
2 teaspoons vanilla extract
1/2 teaspoon salt
Confectioners' sugar for coating

Combine the eggs, sugar, flour, baking cocoa, oil, baking powder, vanilla and salt in a bowl and mix well. Chill in the refrigerator for 8 hours or longer.

Preheat the oven to 350 degrees. Shape the dough into balls. Coat with confectioners' sugar. Place on a cookie sheet and bake for 10 to 12 minutes or until firm. Cool on the cookie sheet for 5 minutes. Remove to a wire rack to cool completely.

Makes 1 to 2 dozen

Raleigh's Best-Ever Cookies

2 cups chunky peanut butter
   (about 18 ounces)
1 cup granulated sugar
1 cup plus 2 tablespoons packed
   brown sugar
3 eggs
1/2 cup (1 stick) butter, softened
2 teaspoons baking soda

3/4 teaspoon light corn syrup
1/4 teaspoon vanilla extract
1/4 teaspoon salt
4 1/2 cups rolled oats
1 (10-ounce) package candy-coated
   milk chocolate pieces
1 cup (6 ounces) semisweet
   chocolate chips

Preheat the oven to 350 degrees. Combine the peanut butter, granulated sugar, brown sugar, eggs, butter, baking soda, corn syrup, vanilla and salt in a mixing bowl and mix well. Mix in the oats. Stir in the candy and chocolate chips.

Drop by heaping tablespoonfuls 2 inches apart onto greased cookie sheets. Place on the center oven rack and bake for 10 to 12 minutes or until golden brown. Cool on the cookie sheets for 5 minutes. Remove to a wire rack to cool completely.

Note: These cookies are so loaded with ingredients they need to be made monster size.

Makes 4 dozen

White Chocolate Key Lime Cookies

2 cups reduced-fat baking mix
2 egg whites
1/3 cup butter or margarine, softened
3/4 cup packed brown sugar
2 tablespoons granulated sugar

1 1/2 teaspoons vanilla extract
1 cup (6 ounces) white
   chocolate chips
1 tablespoon grated Key lime zest

Preheat the oven to 350 degrees. Combine the baking mix, egg whites, butter, brown sugar, granulated sugar and vanilla in a mixing bowl and beat until smooth. Stir in the white chocolate chips and lime zest.

Spoon the dough onto cookie sheets. Bake for 8 to 10 minutes or just until light brown. Cool on the cookie sheets for 5 minutes. Remove to a wire rack to cool completely.

Makes 2 dozen

Frosted Cookie-Party Cookies

Frosted Cookie-Party Cookies
6 cups sifted all-purpose flour
1 teaspoon salt
2 cups (4 sticks) butter, softened
2 cups sugar
4 eggs
2 teaspoons vanilla extract

Cookie Party Frosting
2 egg whites
1/4 tablespoon cream of tartar
1/4 tablespoon vanilla extract
2 1/2 cups sifted confectioners' sugar
Food coloring (optional)

Cookies
Sift the flour and salt together. Cream the butter in a mixing bowl until light. Add the sugar gradually, beating constantly until fluffy. Add the eggs and vanilla and mix well. Add the flour mixture gradually to form a dough, mixing well by hand after each addition. Cover and chill in the refrigerator for 5 hours or longer.

Preheat the oven to 375 degrees. Roll the dough 1/8 inch thick on a lightly floured surface. Cut with a floured cookie cutter and arrange on ungreased cookie sheets. Bake for 10 minutes or until the edges are light brown. Cool on the cookie sheets for 5 minutes. Remove to a wire rack to cool completely.

Frosting
Beat the egg whites with the cream of tartar and vanilla in a mixing bowl until foamy. Add the confectioners' sugar gradually, beating until stiff peaks form. Tint as desired with food coloring. Spread over the cookies. Let stand until firm.

Makes 2 dozen

North Carolina's official song is "The Old North State"; the state bird is the cardinal; the state flower is the dogwood; and the state motto is Esse quam videri—To be, rather than to seem.

Strawberry Shortcake Truffles

1 cup white chocolate candy coating
2/3 cup chopped fresh strawberries
   or thawed drained frozen
   strawberries
Grated zest of 1 orange
3 1/2 cups crumbled yellow cake or
   pound cake, about 11 ounces

1 or 2 drops of red food coloring
   (optional)
2 cups white chocolate candy coating
Sprinkles or dried strawberries, for
   decoration (optional)

Place 1 cup white chocolate candy coating in a medium microwave-safe bowl. Microwave on High for 1 minute or until melted; stir until very smooth. Cool slightly.

Combine the strawberries and orange zest in a food processor or blender and process until puréed. Add the purée gradually to the crumbled cake in a large bowl, mixing well after each addition. Add the melted candy coating and mix well. Stir in the food coloring. Cover with plastic wrap and chill for 1 hour or until firm.

Scoop the truffle mixture by teaspoonfuls and roll gently to form balls. Place on a baking sheet lined with foil. Freeze for 1 hour or until firm enough to dip into the coating.

Place 2 cups white chocolate candy coating in a medium microwave-safe bowl. Microwave on High until melted, stirring every 45 seconds to prevent overheating. Continue stirring until smooth. Use dipping tools or two forks to dip each truffle into the coating; place on the baking sheet. Decorate as desired before the coating sets. Chill the truffles in the refrigerator for 15 minutes or until set before serving.

Note: You can store the truffles in the refrigerator in an airtight container for up to 1 week.

Makes 2 dozen

Graham Cracker Brittle

12 large graham crackers
3/4 cup (11/2 sticks) butter
1/2 cup packed brown sugar
1/8 teaspoon salt

11/2 cups (9 ounces) semisweet
chocolate chips
1/2 to 1 cup chopped nuts (optional)

Preheat the oven to 375 degrees. Arrange a layer of graham crackers in a baking pan lined with foil.

Melt the butter in a saucepan. Add the brown sugar and salt and cook until the brown sugar dissolves, whisking constantly. Pour over the graham crackers. Bake for 10 minutes or until brown and bubbly. Sprinkle with the chocolate chips. Bake for 1 to 2 minutes longer or until the chocolate chips melt; spread evenly over the top. Sprinkle immediately with the nuts.

Cool in the pan on a wire rack for 30 minutes. Chill in the refrigerator for 30 minutes. Break into pieces. Store between waxed paper in an airtight container in the refrigerator.

Makes 50 pieces

Orange Coconut Balls

1/2 cup (1 stick) butter, softened
1 (1-pound) package
confectioners' sugar
1 (12-ounce) package vanilla
wafers, crushed

1 (6-ounce) can frozen orange juice
concentrate, thawed
1 large can flaked coconut

Cream the butter and confectioners' sugar in a mixing bowl until light and fluffy. Add the cookie crumbs and orange juice concentrate; mix well. Shape into balls and roll in the coconut. Place on a baking sheet lined with baking parchment. Chill for 1 hour or longer before serving.

Makes 3 dozen

Chocolate Sauce

1 cup sugar
2¹/₂ tablespoons good-quality
    baking cocoa

3 tablespoons butter
³/₄ cup evaporated milk
1 teaspoon vanilla extract

Mix the sugar and baking cocoa in a small saucepan. Cook over low heat until the sugar dissolves, stirring to mix well. Add the butter and evaporated milk. Increase the heat and bring to a boil. Cook at a rapid boil for 2 minutes, stirring constantly. Remove from the heat and stir in the vanilla. Serve immediately or cool to room temperature and store in the refrigerator to serve later. Reheat to serve.

Makes 1¹/₂ cups

Kahlúa Dip

8 ounces cream cheese, softened
1¹/₄ cups whipped topping
³/₄ cup packed brown sugar
¹/₃ cup Kahlúa

¹/₂ cup finely chopped pecans
Graham crackers, apple slices,
    strawberries and kiwifruit
    for dipping

Combine the cream cheese, whipped topping, brown sugar and Kahlúa in a mixing bowl and beat until fluffy. Fold in the pecans at serving time. Serve with graham crackers, strawberries, kiwifruit and apple slices for dipping.

Serves 14 to 16

Raleigh is home to the North Carolina State Fair, the state's largest event.

Jason Smith

Chef Proprietor, 18 Seaboard

18 Seaboard, Suite 100, Raleigh, North Carolina • 919-861-4318 • www.18seaboard.com

Born in Raleigh, Jason Smith spent the majority of his youth in coastal Wilmington while enjoying his family's roots in the capital city. Both of Jason's grandfathers, as well as Jason's father, made their living working in downtown Raleigh. Greatly influenced by both of his grandmothers' Southern cooking, Jason started cooking in restaurants in Wilmington while still in high school. This hobby soon became a passion, tempered by his lifelong exposure to the fine art of Southern cooking and honed by first-rate culinary training.

Jason's experience has led him to fine establishments like the Magnolia Grill in Durham, Union Square Café and Gramercy Tavern in New York City and the Peninsula Grill in Charleston.

As Chef Proprietor of 18 Seaboard, Jason celebrates straightforward American cuisine with a modestly contemporary edge. By meshing great, reasonably priced North Carolina cuisine with warm hospitality, 18 Seaboard will most certainly leave its mark on the Raleigh restaurant world for years to come.

Jason's mother, Rachel Smith, served as Community Vice President the year the Junior League of Raleigh decided to focus on a child abuse prevention project. The following year, Rachel was chair of the committee that established and created SAFEchild.

Urban Food Group

www.urbanfoodgroup.com

Chef Contributors:

Jeremy Sabo, *Executive Chef, Urban Food Group*   Rob Bland, *Chef de Cuisine, Coquette*
Ian Sullivan, *Chef de Cuisine, Vivace*   Andrew Schaumann, *Vivace Charlotte*

Kevin and Stacey Jennings launched Urban Food Group in 1998 with the opening of Frazier's in Raleigh. Since then, the seasoned restaurateurs have been recognized in *USA Today*, *Bon Appétit*, and *Southern Living* for their savvy restaurant concepts and the excellent quality and superior value delivered at each establishment. In addition to Frazier's, Urban Food Group's neighborhood bistro, they also own the hip, urban Porter's City Tavern, the chic and updated Italian trattoria Vivace and the French brasserie Coquette.

URBAN FOOD GROUP

Tammy Wingo

Owner, Tammy Wingo Photography

919-363-6318 • www.tammywingo.com

Tammy Wingo, a Cary native, has loved photography for as long as she can remember. As a member of the Cary High School Yearbook Club, she knew from an early age that being a photographer was her dream job. While in college she studied art, however, in the end she decided to pursue a "more practical" business degree. After graduation she worked for several years for a pharmaceutical company but her dream of becoming a professional photographer never left her.

When Tammy's twin sons started kindergarten, she decided to pursue her dream and started her own photography business part-time. Soon she had so many clients that she decided to turn her part-time hobby into a full-time venture, and she has never looked back! Initially she focused on weddings, as she loved to tell a story through pictures to document the moments of these special events. Eventually, as her wedding clients started having babies, her business grew to include taking pictures of children. Her business has expanded even further as her clients have asked for her help with commercial projects as well.

Tammy joined the Junior League of Raleigh in 2004 because she wanted to give back to the community. As a member, Tammy shares her photographic talents, documenting the story of what the League does for the community at the Boys and Girls Club, Kids in the Kitchen and more. Her work has been featured in the League's member publication, *the Link*, and has been an integral part of promotional materials for various League events, including Showcase of Kitchens and A Shopping SPREE!

Tammy is a member of White Plains United Methodist Church in Cary. In her spare time, she enjoys photography, painting, dancing, walking and reading. She lives in Apex with her husband, Eric, and her sons, Jack and Benjamin, and their dogs, Ginger and Lucky.

© TAMMY WINGO PHOTOGRAPHY

The contributions of Tammy Wingo, Chef Jason Smith and the Urban Food Group are greatly appreciated.

The Junior League of Raleigh
gratefully acknowledges
the following

Wine and Cheese Sponsors

Picnic with Friends Sponsors

Marie and Scott Abee

Stacy Arch

Lucy and Richard Austin

Mr. and Mrs. Justin Bandholz

Mary Catherine Benson

Cabot Creamery Cooperative

Mr. and Mrs. Samuel B. Cantey IV

Charlotte's Inc.

Anna Baird Choi

Kelly F. Di Domenico

Elaine Miller Collection

Meg and Ed Ergenzinger

Christian A. Hendricks

Katie Hammer Johnson

JLR Headquarters Staff—Joe, Lori, Melanie, Tania and Terri

Hillary and Mark Kokes

Katie Lyon

Melissa Ross Matton

Caroline Miller McEvoy

Alicia and Tyler Morris

North Carolina Museum of Natural Sciences

Dr. and Mrs. William G. Pittman III

Catherine Rideout

Stacey S. Simpson

Dr. and Mrs. Joe Sparks

Jennifer Straw Olson

Meredith D. Taylor, DDS, PA

Lisa Ginger Vanderberry

Whitney and Eric von Haam

Elizabeth Ann Wicker

Virginia and David Yopp

Young, Moore and Henderson, P.A.

Junior League of Raleigh Boards

2007–2008

Linda Brown Douglas *President*
Virginia Yopp *President-elect*
Anna Absher *Community Vice President*
Andrea Fox *Funding & Development Vice President*
Jennifer Doerfler *Membership Vice President*
Whitney von Haam *Communications & Strategies Vice President*
Christian Swain *Training Vice President*
Lisa Marie Ferrell *Nominating Captain*
Jenifer Straw Olson *Secretary*
Beth Lowery *Treasurer*
Jennie Hayman *Sustaining Advisor*
Jill Gammon *Sustaining Advisor*

2008–2009

Virginia Yopp *President*
Melissa Ross Matton *President-elect*
Wendy Webster *Community Vice President*
Catherine Rideout *Funding & Development Vice President*
Kelly Huffstetler *Membership Vice President*
Liza Roney *Communications & Strategies Vice President*
Andrea Fox *Training Vice President*
Gentry Hoffman *Nominating Captain*
Alicia Morris *Secretary*
Heather Horton *Treasurer*
Mary Moss *Sustaining Advisor*
Megg Rader *Sustaining Advisor*

2009–2010

Melissa Ross Matton *President*
Wendy Webster *President-elect*
Stacy Arch *Community Vice President*
Helen Miller *Funding & Development Vice President*
Lisa Vanderberry *Membership Vice President*
Rhonda Beatty *Communications & Strategies Vice President*
Anna Baird Choi *Training Vice President*
Whitney von Haam *Nominating Captain*
Stacey Simpson *Secretary*
Jenni Kinlaw *Treasurer*
Susan McAllister *Sustaining Advisor*

Contributors

We would like to say a heartfelt "thank you" to the people listed below, all of whom in no small way helped to create this cookbook by contributing their recipes, their culinary skills, their taste buds and most importantly their time. A special thank you to the families and friends of everyone listed for supporting the Junior League of Raleigh during this endeavor—without you this book would not have been possible.

Anna Reed Absher
Shelley Earp Aldridge
DeLana M. Anderson
Katherine T. Anderson
Kristen A. Anderson
Molly Smith Anderson
Stacy Andrew Arch
Nina J. Argiry
Rebecca K. Ayers
Alison Tew Bailey
Jennifer L. Baldinelli
Suzanne C. Barnhart
Chris Trotter Bason
Brittany C. Bass
Lainey Milani Bass
Ronda Bazley Moore
Mary Adelaide Bell
Patricia Benedict
Jessica K. Bennett
Conita A. Benson
Kristen D. Bessette
Wynn Thorne Bettinsoli
Jennifer M. Birch
Ashleigh E. Black
Shanah Fuerst Black
Mary M. Blake
Adrienne A. Bohannon
Lee-Ashley Jernigan Bonfield
Melissa B. Boyd
Catherine Boykin
Jessica Lea Bradley
Stewart Bradshaw
Gay S. Bray
Emily J. Brinker
Anna J. Brinkley
Sherri L. Britt
Nancy W. Bromhal
Kathleen Goodwin Brown

Janet K. Brownlee
Marisa Bryant
Ellen Greer Buffaloe
Jessica Dawn Bullock
Lisa K. Bullock
Lisa Burnett
Pam Burr
Lorna R. Butters
Sarah Anne Calhoun
Melissa J. Callaway
Ashley Clark Campbell
Ashley H. Campbell
Ginger P. Caporal
Stacey C. Carothers
Tonya Kelsey Chapman
Anna Baird Choi
Marianna Partrick Clampett
Sarah Lang Clapp
Tracey S. Cloninger
Cindy Sparrow Collett
Candice O. Combs
Gwynne E. Cook
Hazel C. Cooper
Erin Baker Corbett
Nikki Corderman
Caroline H. Corriher
Christy V. Council
Liz W. Coward
Amanda B. Cox
Anna Elizabeth Cox
Freddy V. Cox
Linda Gardner Crandall
Elizabeth H. Creech
Sarah Dalonzo-Baker
Amy C. Darden
Brigid C. Davidson
Amanda M. Davies
Amy Davis

Susan Galyen Deihl
Cheryl G. Dell'Osso
Cynthia Cowling Densmore
Kelly F. Di Domenico
Ana Catherine Dickens
Carolyn Hollis Dickens
Alesia M. Dicosola
Jean (Chip) H. Dodd
Emily A. Doyle
Jennifer Anne Dunn
Nora Duran
Jennifer C. Durbin
Kimberly W. Durland
Missy Hutchins Edlin
Ashleigh Brown Edminster
Ashlegh E. Edwards
Marlet M. Edwards
Tricia Talbert Ellen
Jill Ellison
Michelle H. Emrath
Tanya S. Eney
Meg Tate Ergenzinger
Quinn Etheridge
Jill K. Evans
Elizabeth P. Farrell
Lauren R. Feldman
Katie Feltey
Lisa Marie L. Ferrell
Jocelyn A. Fina
Annette S. Fisher
Cathy Moreland Fleming
Christina W. Floyd
Leigh Forehand
Susan Twiddy Fountain
Ann Marie Fowler
Andrea O. Fox
Emilie R. Foy
Heather E. Frantz

Contributors continued

Amber B. Frasketi
Amanda Fuller
Emily P. Funderburk
Laura Taylor Gable
Jill Gammon
Martha T. Gehring
Phyllis Salerno Gehringer
Heather L. Gibson
Carole C. Gilliam
Jennifer L. Godwin
Katherine Maeve Goff
Sarah L. Goodman
Jennifer Gottsegen
Anna Elizabeth Gould
Cameron Pitts Graham
Danielle R. Grant
M. E. Price Grant
Carrie V. Gray
Emily G. Greene
Charlotte M. Griffin
Emily Irby Grimes
Anne J. Grimm
Amanda B. Guillois
Amy R. Hall
Kerry Hall
Jane Steward Hamlin
Brett Hammond
Cheryl B. Harding
Sue H. Harley
Renee Harris
Katie W. Hartzog
Amelia P. Hayes
Jessica Boyce Hayes
Erin K. Hemminger
Jane Henderson
Liz Ann Henderson
Jennie Rhyne Hendrix
Mary Margaret Hill
Tamma Hill
Wendie Kay Hill
Sara S. Hines
Alyssa O. Hockaday
Mollie L. Hodl
Gentry Summerlin Hoffman
Lisa D. Hollowell

Dena Aretakis Horn
Andria K. Hornaday
Lynne Hornaday
Carrie E. Horton
Donna K. Hovis
Pamela L. Howard
Kathryn A. Hubbard
Kelly Little Huffstetler
Joanna M. Hugo
Kristen M. Humphries
Barbara A. Jackson
Sydney McDaniel Jamison
Kristen Hoffman Janko
Nicole E. Jarvis-Miller
Ginny S. Jenkins
Katie Hammer Johnson
Kelsie J. Johnson
Mary Beth Flynn Jones
Nanda L. Jones
Cathy F. Jordan
Anastasia Marie Judge
Whitner Stewart Kane
Chancy M. Kapp
Amanda Marie Karam
Robin M. Kennedy
Katie Kincaid
Katie King
Jenni Kinlaw
Christy L. Knight
Kelly Kopp
Erin Carnahan Lane
Audrey Lenhausen
Mitzi Renee Levering
Carrie L. Lieb
Stacie York Lindley
Melissa J. Linn
Molly V. Logan
Julia B. Loughren
Joyce Loveless
Tiffany Allison Lund
Katie Lyon
Andrea V. Mace
Ann H. Mailly
Robin White Mangum
Sara Atkins Mann

Shade Elam Maret
Amy H. Marshburn
Jamie Gilbert Martin
Margaret R. Martin
Mary M. Martin
Ann Watters Matteson
Ann W. Matthews
Melissa Ross Matton
Jean D. Maupin
Susan Pate May
Allison McAllister
Caroline V. McCall
Meghan McCleery
Frances S. McClintock
Katie McCollum
Julia Rivenbark McCullough
Shannon McDonald
Quinn W. McFall
Julie L. McGarry
Natalie M. McGowan
Callaway McKay
Elisabeth McMahon
Ashley S. McMillan
Lanier Thomason McRee
Katherine McIntosh Meyer
Erica T. Meyers
Kelly Brannon Miller
Renee Miller
Ashley K. Mills
Kelly A. Mills
Mary Lyons Mitchell
Tracy Moldin Mitchell
Katie Monaghan
Danita Morgan
Alicia Culp Morris
Katrina P. Morrocco
Joyce Moses
Paula E. Murray
Megan N. Muzychka
Amber Ross Myers
Molly Shepherd Nichols
Elisabeth Nixon
Jennifer S. O'Connor
Meghan Leah Odorizzi
Allison M. Olive

Jennifer Straw Olson
Jill Leigh Ovsievsky
Ashley G. Parker
Elizabeth D. Parker
Jamie G. Parsons
Jennifer R. Pate
Ann-Stewart E. Patterson
Suzy T. Pearson
Chemberly Zink Pecze
Tiffany B. Penley
Leigh Arnemann Peplinksi
Donna M. Perry
Kayce Collier Petty
Beverly Phelps
Mary Paige Phillips
Gretchen F. Piechottka
Casey M. Pike
Betsy B. Pittman
Julie F. Ploscyca
Jeannie Holloway Poindexter
Kathryn Poole
Gena S. Poulos
Katherine S. Pretzer
Lisa Venner Price
Kristin P. Prince
Danielle R. Quiocho
Melanie Rankin
Erika Sigrid Rasmussen
Debbie F. Ray
Sara Allison Reason
Violet Barwick Rhinehart
Summer R. Rich
Catherine Davis Rideout
Liz Riley-Young
Dale H. Roane
Anne R. Rogers
Caroline M. Rohs
Liza L. Roney
Annelise Humphries Roper
Jessica K. Ruhle
Amanda Jean Saddler
Gina Rose Sarant
Summey N. Savage
Samantha C. Saxenmeyer
Diane Schabinger

Leslie S. Scheve
Brooke Cornelius Schmidt
Caroline Ballenger Seale
Kristin Seale
Erin C. Seamen
Ashley H. Seamster
Heather Shepherd
Kelly Shoaff
Kim W. Sieredzki
Stacey S. Simpson
Danielle R. Slavin
Alicia H. Smith
Jane S. Smith
Jane L. Smothers
Nancy Sobus
Melissa Sowry
Eva Parks Spero
Maggie A. Spivey
Brantley Springett
Sookia M. Staggers
Judith B. Starritt
Iris A. Stephenson
Elisabeth S. Strickland
Elizabeth K. Strickland
Jennifer Galioto Strickland
Shana M. Stutts
Jessica Elaine Sutton
Ashley Chapman Taylor
Connie M. Teague
Katherine D. Teague
Deanna Brown Tetterton
Sara G. Thomas
Jeanna-Marie Tiller
Kate B. Tillman
Jill Triana
Lauren Trojan
Melanie C. Turner
Amy S. Valerio
Sara S. Van Asch
Lisa Ginger Vanderberry
Lee Veit
Vee Vee Vick
Anna F. Vinson
Whitney von Haam
Emily C. Wade

Kaler E. Walker
Kristen B. Walker
Caroline Coln Wall
Sarah T. Walston
Kimberly M. Watkins
Nancy Elizabeth Watson
Katy A. Waugh
Michelle Oppegaard Weaver
Lexi M. Webster
Lindsay Jones Webster
Wendy L. Webster
Sarah E. Weidaw
Anne Hutchison Wein
Idana D. Weiss
Alison Perkins West
Jennifer L. Westcott
Michelle C. Whichard
Julie Yu Whitlock
Elizabeth Ann Wicker
Kate Hylton Wickers
Stacey Speight Wiley
Pat M. Wilkins
Kimberly Y. Williams
Melanie Williams
Stephanie R. Williams
Lisa M. Williamson
Anna Winifred Wilson
Katie McEwen Wilson
Elaine W. Wood
Jennifer Culberson Wood
Elizabeth Anne Woodrome
Courtney C. Worley
Mary Brent Wright
Parker Watkins Wright
Donna Wynn
Emily Combs Yeatts
Virginia L. Yopp
Nora A. Zarcone
Ginny Zuleba
Team AWCM 2008–09
Team Transfer 2008–09

Please accept our sincerest apologies for anyone we may have accidentally forgotten to mention!

Index

Index continued

Index continued

For additional copies of

You're Invited Back
A Second Helping of Raleigh's Favorite Recipes

please visit our Web site, www.jlraleigh.org,
or call the Junior League of Raleigh at
919-787-7480.